A Shaker Reader

ANTIQUES Magazine Library

AMERICAN AND BRITISH PEWTER
An Historical Survey
Edited by John Carl Thomas

THE ART OF THE POTTER
Redware and Stoneware
Edited by Diana and J. Garrison Stradling

CHINESE EXPORT PORCELAIN
An Historical Survey
Edited by Elinor Gordon

LIGHTING IN AMERICA
From Colonial Rushlights to Victorian Chandeliers
Edited by Lawrence S. Cooke

NEEDLEWORK
An Historical Survey
Edited by Betty Ring

PHILADELPHIA FURNITURE & ITS MAKERS
Edited by John J. Snyder, Jr.

PILGRIM CENTURY FURNITURE
An Historical Survey
Edited by Robert Trent

PORTRAIT PAINTING IN AMERICA
The Nineteenth Century
Edited by Ellen Miles

ANTIQUE METALWARE
Brass, Bronze, Copper, Tin, Wrought & Cast Iron
Edited by James R. Mitchell

A SHAKER READER
Edited by Milton C. and Emily Mason Rose

A Shaker Reader

Edited by
Milton C. and Emily Mason Rose

A Main Street Press Book

Universe Books   New York

Articles included in this volume, or excerpts from such articles, are printed as they appeared in the following issues of *The Magazine* ANTIQUES:

Part I: The Shaker Utopia, October, 1970; The Kentucky Shakers, November, 1947; The Shakers of Maine, June, 1975; Shaker Inspirational Drawings, December, 1945; The Coming Shaker Exhibition in Manhattan, November 1935.

Part II: The Architecture of the Shakers, October, 1957; A Shaker House in Canaan, New York, April, 1962; The Shaker Meetinghouses of Moses Johnson, October, 1970; Micajah Burnett and the Buildings at Pleasant Hill, October, 1970.

Part III: The Shakers in a New World, October, 1957; Craftsmanship of an American Religious Sect, August, 1928; The Furniture of an American Religious Sect, April, 1929; An Interpretation of Shaker Furniture, January, 1933; Unusual Forms in Shaker Furniture, October, 1970; Regional Characteristics of Western Shaker Furniture, October, 1970; The Shaker Furniture of Elder Henry Green, May, 1974.

Part IV: Shaker Crafts on View, October, 1957; Functionalism in Shaker Crafts, October, 1970; Shaker Industries in Kentucky, March, 1974.

Part V: The Shakers Today, October, 1970.

First Edition

Library of Congress Catalog Card Number 77-70773

ISBN 0-87663-969-4, paper
ISBN 0-87663-297-5, cloth

Published by Universe Books
381 Park Avenue South
New York City 10016

Produced by The Main Street Press
42 Main Street
Clinton, New Jersey 08809

Contents

Introduction

The increasing interest in the history of that utopian society properly called The United Society of Believers in Christ's Second Appearing, better known to us as the Shakers, stems from a combination of recently published scholarly works on the origin and early history of the sect, a renewed appreciation of the extraordinary excellence of design and craftsmanship to be found in the furniture, agricultural tools, and household articles which the Shakers produced, and, finally, the recent efforts to acquire, restore, and preserve what remains of their former communities in America. In the mid-nineteenth century these numbered some fifteen to twenty separate, but closely related, settlements containing at their height some five to six thousand believers.

An understanding of the rise of this extraordinary communal sect is aided by some knowledge of the religious motivation which imbued their lives and products with a unique spiritual quality. It is hard for us, so saturated in the twentieth century by secular scientific and industrial endeavors, to realize the depth of the religious, pietistic feeling which swept through parts of Great Britain and continental Europe in the eighteenth century, and gave rise to many new interpretations of the Protestant ethic. Included in these offshoots of Calvinism were the Shaker attempts to return to the tenets of the early apostolic Christian church, and to strive toward a new perfection and harmony through the practice of strict religious beliefs. These beliefs were strongly held and fought for, and much suffering and sacrifice accompanied the struggle. The Puritans led the way to a new promised land in the seventeenth century. Of the many smaller perfectionist groups that followed later, seeking freedom to worship and live as they thought best, the most long-lived was that of the Shakers. They, in turn, were followed by groups whose imaginative and often controversial stirrings could not be accommodated elsewhere. No religious group, however, created an aesthetic as original and compelling as the Shakers. *A Shaker Reader* collects the articles about the Society published in *The Magazine* ANTIQUES over a period of forty-six years, telling some of the story of this amazing sect, and its influence on the world and contemporary ways of thinking and seeing.

In 1928, ANTIQUES, founded six years earlier, published its first article on the Shakers. Interestingly enough, this article was by Edward Deming Andrews and Faith Andrews who had become interested in the Shakers as early as 1923 and continued through the years to do research and to write about these people and their extraordinary lives. The Andrewses compiled a comprehensive collection of the inspirational drawings and other objects encompassing all aspects of Shaker life. Dr. Andrews once spoke of the "inestimable encouragement" given to him and his wife by Homer Eaton Keyes, the first editor of ANTIQUES, when they first became absorbed in the study of the Shakers. He mentioned particularly that Keyes's "imaginative scholarship was always at the service of others." A man of such imagination could foresee, in the early years of the magazine, the tremendous impact that the Shaker culture would have in our own times. Our discovery of the Shakers and their world would have been much delayed had it not been for the Andrewses themselves and for Keyes's interest in their research. They were all inspired by the Shaker concept of design and the fact that it was dependent upon a way of life based upon religious tenets. The number of articles in this collection by the Andrewses attests to their life-long devotion to the Shakers.

The continuing and growing interest in the Believers is reflected in the increasing number of articles pertaining to them and their work to be found in ANTIQUES from 1928 on, through the thirties, forties and fifties, and then burgeoning forth with a whole issue of seven articles in 1970. Homer Eaton Keyes's first interest in the Shakers has been well sustained and developed by the succeeding editors, Alice Winchester and Wendell Garrett.

From these selected articles, extending nearly a half-century, it is interesting to note the extent to which appreciation and comprehension evolved and interest and understanding grew. The recognition of the value of the Shakers' art and artifacts, and particularly their architecture, developed slowly. It seemed to proceed hand in hand with a similar development in the arts and architecture in Europe during the early twentieth century—a turning away from Victorianism and a highly elaborate and decorative style towards a simpler and more utilitarian taste. The Bauhaus led in this movement. In time, the designers of the modern in Europe were to be influenced by Shaker ingenuity and form, especially as it was expressed in work with wood. And in the present day, with a growing need for a simpler life style, we see beauty, economy, and tranquility in the functionalism and austerity of the Shakers' art.

These articles which appeared in the pages of ANTIQUES will arrest the attention both of those already acquainted with the origin and development of the movement, as well as of those who will be concerned to know more of the contribution that this comparatively long-lived sect made to our nineteenth-century society.

While it is true, as has been noted, that the Shaker movement was born in England late in the eighteenth century, it is also true that its great growth occurred only after its transplanting to the New World during the early years of the following century. The United States, therefore, is the only place where preservation of originally-sited communities can be found. It is fortunate that this fact has been realized by a few far-sighted individuals, such as Mrs. Lawrence K. Miller, who has been so imaginative and determined in her efforts to secure the settlement at Hancock, Massachusetts, for future generations. The response that her tireless efforts have received is a clear indication of the growing realization of the historical importance of assuring future accessibility to Shaker thought and practice. It is, moreover, the means of preserving for future interest and enjoyment the remaining examples of architecture and crafts which these extraordinary people created. All of this has been keenly felt and the measures adopted hold promise of securing, for future generations, a better understanding of the Shakers as well as an appreciation of their work.

Museums and Public Collections

Compiled by The Shaker Museum Foundation, Inc., Old Chatham, New York, 1976.

DELAWARE

The Henry Francis du Pont Winterthur Museum, Winterthur. 19735

Off State Rte. 52. Shaker storage-walls, woodwork, furniture, baskets, boxes and fabrics are displayed in a recreated dwelling room and storage room. The two rooms may be seen on museum tours for which reservations are required. Museum closed on national holidays. *Fee.* Tel. (302) 656-8591.

KENTUCKY

Kentucky Museum, Bowling Green. 42101

Kentucky Building, Rte. U.S. 68 on Western Kentucky University Campus. Bruch MacLeish, curator of collections. Collection of Kentuckiana, including South Union Shaker furniture, tools, and crafts. Monday-Friday, 9-4:30; Saturday, 11-3; Sunday, 2-4; during university vacations, open on a limited schedule. No fee. Tel. (502) 745-2592.

Shakertown at Pleasant Hill, Inc., Harrodsburg. 40330
Rte. U.S. 68, 25 miles southwest of Lexington. James C. Thomas, president. A restored Shaker village of which 27 original buildings remain; finest remaining Shaker site in the South. Museum in the Centre Family Dwelling contains furniture in original settings, costumes, shops, and artifacts, largely of Pleasant Hill. Trustees' House with famous twin spiral stairs; meetinghouse. Dining and overnight lodgings available in original buildings. Daily, 9-5. Fee. Tel. (606) 734-5411.

Shakertown at South Union. 42283
Rte. U.S. 68 and Ky. 73, 15 miles west of Bowling Green, 3 miles east of Auburn. Mrs. Curry Hall, director. A large collection of Shaker furniture, crafts, and textiles housed in the 1824 Centre House. Open Mother's Day to Labor Day, Monday through Saturday, 9-5; Sunday, 1-5. Weekends during September and October. During winter by appointment for groups. Fee. Tel. (502) 542-4720.

MAINE
Shaker Museum, Sabbathday Lake Shaker Community. 04274
Poland Spring, 23 miles north of Portland. Maine Turnpike to Gray, exit 11, north 8 miles on Rte. 26. Theodore E. Johnson, director. An original Shaker village founded in 1793 and still occupied by Shaker sisters. Gift shop sells Shaker-made items and is open year around, Sunday excepted. Museum open to visitors only in the summer. Extensive collection of Shaker manuscripts available for research purposes. Museum hours: May 30 to Labor Day, Monday-Saturday, 10-4:30; closed Sunday. Fee. Tel. (207) 926-4597.

MASSACHUSETTS
Boston Museum of Fine Arts. 02115
465 Huntington Avenue, Back Bay. Shaker recreated room with furniture, artifacts. Tuesday-Sunday, 10-5; Tuesday evenings until 9; closed Mondays, Thanksgiving, Christmas, New Year's, July 4. Fee, Tuesday-Sunday, except half-price Tuesday evenings and Sundays. No fee for children under 16. Tel. (617) 267-9300.

Fruitlands Museums, Harvard. 01451
Rte. 110, side road to the left, north of Harvard village. William Henry Harrison, director. One of five museums on the grounds, the Shaker house (moved in from the Harvard Shaker community) contains furniture, costumes, textiles, artifacts, etc., largely from Harvard. Extensive collection of manuscripts available for research purposes. May 30-September 30, Tuesday-Sunday, 1-5. Fee. Tel. (617) 456-3924.

Hancock Shaker Community, Inc. 01201
Rte. U.S. 20, 5 miles west of Pittsfield. Mrs. Lawrence K. Miller, president; John H. Ott, director. A former Shaker village now under restoration; 17 original buildings, including the famous Round Barn. Shaker furniture, costumes, artifacts, industrial exhibits. June 1-October 31, daily 9:30-5. Fee. Tel. (413) 443-0188; also, 447-7284.

NEW HAMPSHIRE
Canterbury Shaker Museum, East Canterbury. 03224
Located 13.5 miles northeast of Concord; Rtes. U.S. 4 and 202, 4 miles to Rte. 106; bear left 6.5 miles, then turn left on road marked "Shaker Village" 3 miles. Charles F. Thompson, director. An original Shaker village founded in 1792 and still occupied by Shaker sisters. Gift shop sells Shaker-made items. Museum hours from May 25 to 3rd Saturday of October, Tuesday-Saturday. Tours every hour on the hour, 9-4. Labor Day to October 12 by appointment only. Closed Sunday, Monday. Fee. Tel. (603) 783-9822.

NEW YORK
Shaker Museum, Old Chatham. 12136
Located 5 miles from exit B-2 of the Berkshire spur of the New York Thruway; 17 miles from Albany on Rte. U.S. 20, turn south on Rte. 66 and follow signs. Robert F. W. Meader, director. Oldest and largest of the public museums devoted to Shaker crafts; 36 galleries housing 18,000 objects. Furniture, crafts, inventions, costumes, fabrics, complete shops, industries. Herb Shop from Enfield, Conn. Extensive collections of Shaker books and manuscripts available for research purposes. May 1-October 31 daily, 10-5:30; library available for research throughout year upon application. Fee. Tel. (518) 794-9105; if no answer, 794-9100.

OHIO
Dunham Tavern Museum, Cleveland. 44106
6709 Euclid Avenue. Mrs. Harold M. Witsie, curator. Recreated Shaker room. Daily all year, 12:30-4:30, except Mondays and holidays. No fee. Tel. (216) 431-1060.

Golden Lamb Hotel, Lebanon. 45036
27-31 South Broadway, on Rte. 63 between I-71 and I-75, Ohio's oldest hostelry. Jackson B. Reynolds, director. Hotel is richly furnished with antiques, many Shaker. Authentic Shaker bedroom and Shaker Goodroom (pantry). Shaker dining room for the public. No fee. Tel. (513) 932-5065.

Kettering-Moraine Museum, Kettering. 45439
35 Moraine Circle South, West Stroop Street and Kettering Boulevard. Mr. Richard R. Hunt, director. Local history; Shaker room dedicated to the Watervliet, Ohio, community. Currently, Sundays only, 1-5. No fee. Tel. (513) 299-2722; if no answer, (513) 299-0594.

Shaker Historical Society Museum, Shaker Heights. 44120
16740 South Park Blvd. Shaker furniture, crafts, and industries, largely from the North Union community. Some manuscripts. Miss Suzanne B. Toomey, director. Tuesday-Friday, 2-4; Sunday, 2-5; closed Monday and Saturday.

Warren County Historical Society Museum, Lebanon. 45036
105 South Broadway, on Rte. 63 between I-71 and I-75; two doors south of the Golden Lamb Hotel. Mrs. Elva R. Adams, director. Shaker furniture and crafts largely from Union Village displayed in one room and one gallery. Tuesday-Saturday, 9-4; Sunday, 12-4. Fee. Tel. (513) 932-1817.

Western Reserve Historical Society, Cleveland. 44106
10825 East Boulevard. Meredith B. Colket, Jr., director. Shaker furniture, crafts, and inventions displayed in the Shaker Room. Largest and finest collection of Shaker books and manuscripts in the world available for research purposes. Tuesday-Saturday, 10-5; Sunday, 2-5. Closed on national holidays. Fee. Tel. (216) 721-5722.

PENNSYLVANIA
Philadelphia Museum of Art. 19130
Benjamin Franklin Parkway at 26th St. Exhibit of Shaker furniture, artifacts. The Zieget collection was given in the spring of 1977 by Mr. and Mrs. Julius Zieget and their daughter, Marcia Zieget Reiger. (Apply at desk for admittance). Daily 9-5; closed on national holidays. No fee on Sunday mornings and Mondays. Other days, fee. Tel. (215) 763-8100.

VERMONT
Shelburne Museum, Shelburne. 05482
Rte. U.S. 7, 7 miles south of Burlington. Sterling D. Emerson, director. Shaker artifacts in Shaker shed from Canterbury, N.H. May 15-October 15. Daily, 9-5. Fee. Tel. (802) 985-3344.

WISCONSIN
Milwaukee Art Centre: Villa Terrace. 53202
2220 North Terrace Ave. Tracy Atkinson, director. January-March, Saturday, Sunday 1-5; April-June, September-December, Wednesday, Saturday, Sunday, 1-5; closed holidays. July and August, Wednesday through Sunday, 1-5. No fee except for tours, by appointment. Tel. (414) 271-3656, (414) 271-9508, and 273-7290.

ENGLAND
The American Museum in Britain, Claverton Manor. Bath BA2 7BD

Train from London, 1³/₄ hr., hourly; 2 hrs. by road (M4), 2¹/₂ miles from center of Bath. Ian McCallum, director. Twenty galleries of Americana, including a Shaker room; Mt. Vernon rose garden; herb garden and shop. Last Saturday of March through last Saturday of October. Daily except Monday, 2-5 p.m.; on bank holidays, 12-5 p.m. Fee. Tel. Bath 60503.

*Museum devoted exclusively to Shaker artifacts.

Libraries

In addition to the above listed museums, the following institutions are depositories for significant Shaker materials.

CONNECTICUT

Connecticut State Library, Hartford. 06115
231 Capitol Avenue. Monday-Friday, 8:30-5:00; Saturday, 9-1 (except holiday weekends). Closed Sundays and holidays. Large collection of Enfield, Connecticut, miscellaneous pamphlets. Tel. (203) 566-4777.

DISTRICT OF COLUMBIA

Library of Congress
Books in the general collections; special materials in the rare book, manuscript, and music divisions in Annex. Tel. (202) 426-5000.

INDIANA

Indiana Historical Society Library, Indianapolis. 46204
140 North Senate Avenue. Monday-Friday, 9-5; Saturday, 9-12 (except June-August). West Union material. Tel. (317) 633-4976.

KENTUCKY

Filson Club, Louisville. 40203
118 West Breckinridge Street. Monday-Friday, 9-5; Saturday, 9-12 (except July, August and September). Pleasant Hill material. Apply to Martin F. Schmidt, librarian. Tel. (502) 582-3727.

Kentucky Library, Bowling Green. 42101
Kentucky Building, Rte. U.S. 68, on Western Kentucky University campus. Kentuckiana research collection, especially rich in South Union Shaker manuscripts. Monday-Friday, 8-5; Saturday, 9-4:30; closed Sunday. During university vacations, open on a limited schedule. Apply to Riley Handy, librarian. Tel. (502) 745-2592.

University of Kentucky, Margaret I. King Library, Lexington. 40506
Off Rose Street, opposite Columbia Avenue. Closed Thanksgiving, Christmas and New Year's Days, and Memorial Day. Most materials are in the special collections department. Hours: Monday-Friday, 8-5; Saturday, 8-noon. Apply to head of special collections. Tel. (606) 258-8611.

MASSACHUSETTS

† American Antiquarian Society, Worcester. 01609
185 Salisbury Street, corner of Park Avenue. Monday-Friday, 9-5, except legal holidays. Outstanding collection of Shaker imprints and ancillary materials; manuscript holdings not strong. Apply to Frederick E. Bauer, associate librarian. Tel. (617) 755-5221.

Berkshire Athenaeum, Pittsfield. 01201
1 Wendell Avenue. Monday-Friday, 9-9; Saturday, 9-6. June 15-September 15: Monday, Wednesday, Friday, 9-9; Tuesday, Thursday, Saturday, 9-6. Much Hancock material. Apply to Robert G. Newman, librarian. Tel. (413) 442-1559.

Massachusetts Historical Society, Boston. 02215
1154 Boylston Street. Monday-Friday, 9-4:45. Russell W. and Martha T. Knight Shaker Library. Fine collection of books and pamphlets; few manuscripts. Apply to John D. Cushing, librarian. Tel. (617) 536-1608.

† Williams College, Sawyer Library, Williamstown. 01267
Off Rte. 2, in center of campus. Monday-Friday, 8-5, 7-11; Saturday, 9-5; Sunday, 3-6, 7-11. During college vacations: Monday-Friday, 9-5; closed weekends. Particularly strong in Shaker music, imprints. Apply to Lawrence E. Wikander, librarian. Tel. (413) 597-2502.

MICHIGAN

† *University of Michigan, William L. Clements Library, Ann Arbor. 48109*
South University Avenue. Monday-Friday, 9-5. Apply to H. H. Peckham, director. Tel. (313) 764-2347.

NEW HAMPSHIRE

New Hampshire Historical Society Library, Concord. 03301
30 Park Street, behind State House. Monday-Friday, 9-4:30. Wednesdays to 8 p.m. Tel. (603) 225-3381.

NEW YORK

† *Buffalo and Erie County Public Library, Buffalo. 14203*
Lafayette Square. Rare Book Room. Monday-Friday, 9:30-5. Apply to William H. Loos, curator, rare book room. Tel. (716) 856-7525, ext. 244.

Hofstra University Library, Hempstead, Long Island. 11550
1000 Fulton Avenue. Special collections, 9th floor. Tel. (516) 560-3440.

*† *New York Public Library, New York City. 10018*
5th Avenue and 42nd Street. Special collections; manuscript and archives division. Monday, Wednesday, Friday, Saturday, 10-6. Apply to the executive officer, the research libraries administrative office. Tel. (212) 790-6254.

New York State Library, Albany. 12224
State Education Building, Washington Avenue opposite Capitol. General reference and four subsidiary divisions. Monday-Friday, 8:30-6 (except 5 on the eve of a holiday); closed Saturday and Sunday, national and state holidays. All section libraries close at 5 p.m. Apply to Robert P. Stewart, principal librarian, readers' services. Tel. (518) 474-7451.

Syracuse University, George Arents Research Library, Syracuse. 13210
Monday-Friday, 8:30-5; Saturday by appointment, except legal holidays. Approximately 300 titles and growing, no mss. Apply to Miss Ruth Salisbury, rare book librarian. Tel. (315) 476-5541.

NORTH CAROLINA

Duke University, William R. Perkins Library, Durham. 27706
Monday-Friday, 8 a.m.-11 p.m.; Saturday, 8 a.m.-6 p.m.; Sunday, 2-11 p.m. Closed Thanksgiving, Christmas and New Year's Days. Schedule varies during summer sessions and interim periods. Apply to Connie R. Dunlap, university librarian. Tel. (919) 684-2034.

OHIO

Dayton and Montgomery County Public Library, Dayton. 45402
215 East 3rd Street. Monday-Friday, 9-9; Saturday, 9-6. Closed Sundays and major holidays. Tel. (513) 224-1651.

Ohio Historical Society Library, Columbus. 43211
1982 Velma Avenue. Monday-Saturday, 9-5. Apply to Paul F. Hill, head librarian. Tel. (614) 469-2064.

WISCONSIN

State Historical Society of Wisconsin, Madison. 53706
816 State Street. Monday-Friday, 8 a.m.-10 p.m.; Saturday, 8-5. Hours vary with the academic year. Tels. (608) 262-9590 (reference librarian); (608) 262-9576 (manuscript librarian).

* Denotes outstanding collection of Shaker books and manuscripts.
† Prior application required for use of materials. *Prospective users of these materials should remember that, since these books and manuscripts are excessively rare and irreplaceable, no withdrawals are permitted nor interlibrary loans arranged.*

I Shakers in the New World

One draws from the articles contained in this section a survey of American utopian experiments originating in England during the latter part of the eighteenth century. The Shaker movement reached its zenith in America in the early and middle years of the following century. Thereafter, it declined until today little remains but the records and history of an interesting social and religious experiment and an important heritage of excellent design—ingenious and simple articles of daily use which were the product of dedicated and divinely-inspired craftsmen. In particular, the development of the Shaker idea in Kentucky and in Maine is treated in this section with illustrations showing the design of the buildings and some of the furniture from those settlements. In Charles Upton's "The Shaker Utopia" we are given the history and religious background of the Shakers. This article is illustrated by photographs of Hancock Shaker Village, mostly taken and captioned by Eugene Merrick Dodd, then curator at Hancock. The Shaker belief in divine inspiration is interpreted in Edward Deming Andrews' survey of Shaker inspirational drawings, and the illustrations of these are most enlightening.

A quotation from a Shaker work entitled *The Millennial Church,* Part II, Chapter V, pp. 83–84, found at the end of the second Andrewses' article, expresses the Society's overriding ethic which informed all of their work:

> God has created man an active, intelligent Being, possessing important powers and faculties, capable of serving himself according to his needs and circumstances; and he is required to devote these powers and faculties to the service of God.

Hancock Shaker Village.

The Shaker utopia

BY CHARLES W. UPTON

HUMAN HISTORY IS replete with myths of utopias or societies enjoying a perfect state of mutual harmony and individual happiness. When the word utopia was coined by Sir Thomas More in 1516 to describe the fabled island where righteousness prevailed and man lived in freedom, prosperity, and justice, he composed it of the Greek words *ou* and *topos,* whose literal translation is "no place." Century after century literature, philosophy, and religion pursued the utopian theme in discussion of the golden age, the Promised Land, the New Atlantis, the millennium, and the New Jerusalem, to mention only a few. These stories of heavens on earth kept alive the hope and conviction that the perfect society was a realizable dream, the more so when existence became unbearably cruel and insupportable.

The history of American utopian experiments or socialism, although largely governed by indigenous forces, has been greatly influenced by European developments and foreign philosophers. In the realm of theory, scholars and reformers were familiar with the egalitarian implications of Christian teachings and the communism of the primitive church, Plato's blueprint of the ideal state in his *Republic,* and Sir Thomas More's fascinating and attractive depiction

of perfect human happiness. The basic drive, however, behind the search for an earthly paradise was to be found in the political, economic, and social disintegration in western Europe at various stages in the transformation from medieval to modern, in the great social upheavals that followed the rise of heretical sects, the Protestant Reformation, the Counter Reformation, the Cromwellian revolution in England, and the French Revolution, together with the massive abuses of the new industrial and urban movement of the eighteenth century. More or less of necessity proposals for reform took on the character of dissent and revolution, a challenge to the Establishment, and those who sought to put these theories into practice were looked upon as enemies of the church or state and treated harshly by their neighbors and the authorities. Such repressive measures inevitably turned the attention of the utopia-minded to America, principally the United States.

After the American Revolution had transformed the American colonies into the United States, the new nation offered, or appeared to offer, unlimited opportunities for the establishment of utopian experiments. Here existed all the ingredients for a perfect society—political and religious freedom, cheap land, an open society, and the prospect of early riches for the earnest and hard-working immigrant. In addition to the almost unlimited amount of virgin soil which allowed location of new settlements either on the frontier or close to the more populous areas, the United States presented a most favorable environment for a new moral code, a new economy, and a new and more perfect form of human association. Equally important, the violence and radicalism of the American Revolution which had broken the chains of religious orthodoxy and economic conservatism were reinforced by the spirit of freedom and equality of the frontier. Beginning in the early 1800's the United States was in the throes of a social and political revolution later described as the age of the common man. A wave of unrest swept across the country, particularly the eastern states, as religious revivalism and Jeffersonian democracy made steady headway against Calvinist doctrine and Federalist politics. A spirit of optimism spread throughout the population, arousing new hopes and expectations of well-being and progress and constituting a most favorable background for new and extreme proposals for social experiments.

During the nineteenth century over a hundred thousand men, women, and children, repelled and discouraged by economic and social misery and the hostility of their neighbors, fled to America to set up more than a hundred model communities. Because they were faced with a shortage of capital, burdened with numbers of poor persons immediately concerned with economic security and compelled to accept leadership of a few strong personalities, these individuals found it necessary to adopt communism in one form or another. Only by combining their scanty resources could they purchase the large tracts of land needed for an agricultural existence and maintain the controls needed to combat individualism, dissension, laziness, and backsliding. In a number of instances these sects had adopted communistic principles before coming to America; other groups not originally communistic became so for social and economic reasons; and in some instances communism became an end in itself. Another characteristic of these colonies, particularly the pietistic types, was the desire to separate themselves from established (wicked) society. This relative isolation permitted them to practice any special principles, such as celibacy, in relative safety, and also protected the members against the temptations and contamination of the outside world. Millennialism, or belief in the imminent thousand-year reign of Jesus Christ, was another widely shared belief.

The United Society of Believers in Christ's Second Appearing, as the Shakers officially called themselves, is by all tests the most extensive, the most enduring, and for the American people the most important communal sect. The Shakers, English pietists, developed out of English Quakerism and distantly from the Camisards. Jane and James Wardley were leaders of a Manchester sect derisively called Shaking Quakers or Shakers because of their frenzied physical manifestations of religious zeal. Ann Lee joined this group in 1758 and became the accepted head in 1770 after a short stay in the Manchester jail for Sabbath-breaking. There Christ appeared to her and explained the cause of human depravity to be the sex act. Mother Ann, as she was now called, preached her gospel of sinlessness and celibacy, and sought unsuccessfully to recruit new members. After four years in which she was accused of blasphemy, tried and acquitted before an Anglican (church) court, imprisoned

Interior, Round Stone Barn, Hancock Shaker Village. This octagonal framework, running from the floor of the manger to the cupola, is an air shaft for ventilating the hay which was piled around it. The beams of the roof enclose the barn's twelve-sided superstructure; many of the beams are split halfway down their length to provide economical support for the roof's outer edge.

and stoned along with her companions, Ann was directed in a vision to go to America, where the Church of Christ's Second Appearing would be founded.

Ann and eight followers arrived in New York City on August 6, 1774, after a voyage of three months. Several of the little group sought employment outside the city while Mother Ann found work as a laundress and cared for her ailing husband. John Hocknell, the only person of substantial means among the Shakers, went up the Hudson to Albany where he purchased several hundred acres of wilderness land near the village of Niskayuna from Stephen Van Rensselaer in February 1776. Mother Ann and the others joined him in the spring, almost two years after arriving in the New World.

For several years the tiny group labored to build log cabins, drain and clear the land, and prepare for the converts to Shaker gospel. At first Ann and her disciples enjoyed little success in persuading their neighbors to join them, and they momentarily fell into the clutches of the law when as English newcomers they were suspected of being spies for George III. The turning point in their fortunes came in 1779 when a series of religious revival meetings was held at New Lebanon, New York. These attracted hundreds of people living in towns on the Massachusetts-New York border who heard for the first time of the Shakers at nearby Niskayuna. Many of these traveled there to learn of the new Messiah. Beginning in 1780 Ann and her followers visited New Lebanon and neighboring towns making hundreds of converts. Later in 1781 she and her brother undertook a two-year missionary journey into Massachusetts and Connecticut where they encountered rough handling by the mobs that turned out to greet the leaders of this queer sect. Mother Ann and her brother, William Lee, died the year after their return home in 1784. It is believed that the injuries received in this visitation contributed to Ann's demise at the age of forty-eight.

Fortunately, strong new leaders appeared in the persons of James Whittaker, Joseph Meacham, and Lucy Wright in the crucial years from 1784 to 1821 and of Frederick W. Evans from 1836 to 1893. Three Shaker communities

View of Hancock Shaker Village, showing (from the left) part of the Laundry and Machine Shop, the Brick Dwelling, the small brick Wash House (c. 1810), and the Sisters' Shop (c. 1820). The bushes along the fence are *Rosa gallica officinalis,* the blossoms of which were used for making the Shakers' celebrated rose water.

The Shakers' belief in the separation —though equality—of the sexes is expressed architecturally by this pair of doorways leading into the dining room of the Brick Dwelling at Hancock: that on the right was used by the brethren, that on the left by the sisters. Of pine and butternut, the woodwork is stained a light brown, effectively contrasting with the whitewashed plaster of the walls. The built-in cupboards flanking the doorways are a ubiquitous feature of Shaker interiors, effectively symbolizing the Shakers' insistence on order and tidiness.

were established in New York State, four in Massachusetts, one in Connecticut, two in New Hampshire, and two in Maine. Four groups settled in Ohio, two in Kentucky, and one in Indiana. There were also two short-lived communities in Florida and Georgia.

Converts to Shakerism numbered in the thousands; it is estimated that at the height of the movement some six thousand inhabited the nineteen communities. Shaker religious doctrine was easily reconciled with that of most Protestant sects which involved acceptance of the Bible as the source of all religious teachings, confession of sin, belief in life after death, and a rigid code of individual virtuous conduct leading to perfectionism. Mother Ann's personal contributions to Shaker theology were her belief that God is a dual personality, feminine as well as masculine, and her demand for celibacy to insure purity and spirituality. While Ann herself was endowed with the spirit of Christ, she was not divine, but only the instrument for the expression of divine truth. As for the faithful, life must be lived in accord with the twelve virtues: faith, hope, honesty, continence, conscience, simplicity, meekness, humility, prudence, patience, thankfulness, and charity.

The Shakers' economic growth and well-being were exceptional during the period down to the Civil War. Communism, the antithesis of individual ownership, provided the inspiration for personal benevolence and dedication to group welfare, encouraged the acceptance of discipline needed to maintain the maximum production of goods, and strengthened the authority of the leadership of this tightly knit organization. From the beginning, the Shakers carried on diversified agriculture as the means of livelihood most likely to preserve the communitarian principle. Driven by their religion to economize on time and labor, the Shakers displayed great ingenuity in inventing labor-saving devices

and instituting co-operative production, in some instances approximating the mass-production techniques developed elsewhere later in the century. Meticulous in maintaining high standards of quality, scrupulously honest and fair in pricing, the Shakers produced goods eagerly bought by the outside world, with the result that wealth and prosperity along with an exceptional reputation for integrity blessed the Shaker societies.

Shaker life tended to be standardized in the various communities. Celibacy and communism required strict discipline. Most buildings, including the meetinghouses, had two entrances, one for men, the other for women; separate stairways led to the sleeping quarters, and men and women dined at separate tables in the same room. Order and cleanliness pervaded the shops and dwellings, and the rooms were lined with rows of pegs on which to hang chairs and wearing apparel. Temperance and often total abstinence, along with a moderate use of tobacco, were customary; some families practiced vegetarianism. Visitors, including almost every celebrity, domestic and foreign, came to see communism in action and to watch the Shaker services with their songs, lively dances, marches, and prayers. Curious travelers came to sample the bountiful meals served by the Shaker sisters. All in all it was a busy life with security, simplicity, and satisfaction in settlements of unconscious architectural beauty.

The peak of wealth, membership, and achievement which the Shakers had reached shortly before the Civil War could not be maintained. The losses of property in Kentucky in the war, the inability of Shaker industry to maintain its early advantage of large-scale production, the materialism of the last quarter of the nineteenth century, the failure to hold young members of the order, and the decline in organizational and leadership qualities, along with the ad-

Eldresses' Sitting Room, Meetinghouse, Hancock Shaker Village. The Shaker Ministry, consisting of two Elders and two Eldresses, occupied quarters apart from the rank and file of Believers on the second floor of the meetinghouse. This room adjoins the Eldresses' "retiring" room. The chest of drawers, from the Shaker community at Mount Lebanon, New York, was formerly in the collection of the painter Charles Sheeler. *Photograph by Louis H. Frohman.*

Laundry and Machine Shop, Hancock Shaker Village. Dating in part from 1790, this building is one of the oldest in the Village. It also houses the Village's herb department.

Brethren's Shop, Hancock Shaker Village, c. 1820; one of several similar structures housing the community's varied industries. It now contains exhibitions relating to some of the Shakers' best-known manufactures: chairs, brooms, baskets, and clocks. Visitors to Shaker communities during the nineteenth century marveled at the well-lighted and well-equipped workrooms where the sect's industries were carried on.

Brick Dwelling, Hancock Shaker Village. Built in 1830, this structure was designed to house most of the adult Shakers of the Church Family. In addition to the Family's communal rooms —the kitchen and ancillary storage rooms, the dining room, and the meeting room used for weekday worship— the building contains on its second and third floors the brethren's and sisters' "retiring" rooms. Virtually all the materials used in the building were village-produced: the brick from its brickyard, the wood from its timber lots, the limestone from its quarries.

vancing age of the Shakers, led to an inevitable decline in the economic activity and prosperity of the communities and their members. Slowly the societies, first in the West and then in the East, closed and sent their members to the more populous orders. In 1970 only two communities remain, one at Sabbathday Lake, Maine, and the other at Canterbury, New Hampshire. Here some fifteen sisters carry on as Mother Ann directed. Their chief activity is to welcome visitors from far and near, curious to learn the mysteries of the once-flourishing utopia of Shakerdom.

Other socialistic utopias, co-operative associations, and semicommunistic experiments, however, were set up in the United States and elsewhere after the Civil War, and indeed continue to be founded. For the most part they have not succeeded to the same degree as the early religious groups. Land is no longer cheap, the expense of establish-

ing manufactures is prohibitive, the primitive faith and moral purpose of the early communitarians seem to have disappeared, while capitalism has softened its image by accepting many semisocialistic reforms. Still the search for utopia with its perfect state of human happiness goes on in literaure and social experimentation. B. F. Skinner's *Walden Two* blueprints a scientifically controlled society, while the Israeli *Kibbutzim* and even the hippie communes seek to recapture something of earlier, happier, and more humane life.

All the illustrations here are of Hancock Shaker Village in Massachusetts, which has been restored since 1960; captions are by Eugene Merrick Dodd, curator of the Village. Except as noted, photographs are also by Mr. Dodd.

DINING TABLE AND CHAIRS. Used at the Pleasant Hill colony. The date *June 1868* is painted on the table. Length of table, 9 feet 7 inches.

THE KENTUCKY SHAKERS

By EDWARD DEMING ANDREWS

The unique contribution cf the Shaker sect to American craftsmanship has been made familiar to collectors largely through the writings of Edward D. Andrews, author of numerous articles in ANTIQUES *and other publications and, with his wife, of the book* Shaker Furniture. *Most "Shaker antiques" are from New York and New England, where the movement existed longest: here Mr. Andrews tells of the activities of the Believers who carried their traditions west of the mountains.*

TWO COMMUNITIES of Believers in Christ's Second Appearing, commonly called Shakers, were established in Kentucky in the early years of the nineteenth century. They were founded by missionaries from the parent Shaker colony at New Lebanon, New York, which had been organized in the 1780's.

Reports of a religious revival in the regions north and south of the Ohio River had convinced the presiding ministry at New Lebanon that this area would be a fertile field for the establishment of Shaker colonies. Accordingly, on the first day of the year 1805, three of the sect's ablest preachers, Benjamin S. Youngs, Issachar Bates, and John Meacham, were dispatched to carry to the western frontier the Shaker doctrines of celibacy, confession of sin, separation from the world, and community of goods. They traveled on foot, with a horse to carry their baggage. With no precise destination in mind, they made their way through Washington into Virginia. There they learned from travelers of a sect called "Christians" that manifested phenomena of whirling, jerking, and trembling somewhat like the dancing and "exercises" of the Shakers themselves. Crossing over into Tennessee, they visited one of these Christian settlements at Bull's Gap. Believing, however, that the center of the Revival lay rather in Ohio and Kentucky, they pressed on to a "New Light" colony at Paint Lick, Kentucky. Here they attempted to preach the Shaker doctrines, but were branded as "false prophets" who were out to disrupt the sacred institutions of marriage and private property. Not until they

reached the home oi Malcolm Worley, a prominent leader of the Revival, at Turtle Creek in southern Ohio, did they feel that a promising opening was at hand. A Shaker colony was established there in June 1805, and others followed in Ohio and Indiana.

Work was advanced also in Kentucky. Bates speaks of traveling "this wild wooden world by day and night," carrying on the battle of the spirit against "the doleful works of the flesh." A colony was established at Pleasant Hill between Harrodsburg and Lexington in 1806, and another at Gasper Springs, or South Union, between Bowling Green and Russellville, in 1807. Landholders as well as poor whites and blacks "opened their minds," and bequeathed their worldly goods to the "one true faith." The nucleus of the Pleasant Hill community was the grant of a 140-acre farm by Elisha Thomas, and that at South Union the dedication of all his holdings by Jesse McComb.

SHIRRED RUG. From Pleasant Hill. Made of homespun wool, linsey woolsey, and cotton of many colors, cut in strips, folded, and shirred.

1947

16

These Kentucky communities were representative of the complex but fully integrated social organization of the Shaker church, having distinct customs and dress, architecture and industry, and a craftsmanship characterized by functionalism, simplicity, and an instinct for form. Up to the time of the Civil War and the impact of the machine age, Shaker communities were largely self-sufficient, with dependence on the outside world reduced to a minimum. The two Kentucky colonies attained their greatest membership in the decade 1830–1840.

The basis of Shaker economy was agriculture. Both Pleasant Hill, with more than 4,000 acres of land, and South Union with some 6,000, were famous for their stock and produce. The English socialist, John Finch, wrote in 1844 that "the Shaker land [at Pleasant Hill] is easily known by its superior cultivation and by its substantial stone-wall fences. There are many large, handsome, hewn-stone and brick houses, farm buildings, manufactories, and workshops, all in the neatest order, some of the best in Kentucky."

The Shakers designed, constructed, and furnished their own buildings. Those at Pleasant Hill, of stone and brick, had the trim, unadorned beauty of all Shaker dwellings, with the customary double entrances, one for the brethren and one for the sisters, but they also had arched doorways and spiral staircases of faultless workmanship. Joiners' shops turned out chairs (side and arm, with rockers for the aged and infirm), cases of drawers, chests, beds, tables, benches, adjustable wall brackets for candles — all simple,

 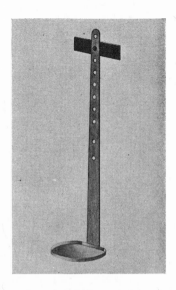

SLAT-BACK CHAIR. Characteristic Shaker form, but with more elaborate turnings than made in the East. CANDLE BRACKET. Made at Pleasant Hill. Of poplar, adjustable by means of holes by which it is hung from a wooden wall peg. Length, 30 inches.

CUPBOARD with pierced tin panels. Used at the South Union colony. Of poplar painted "Shaker blue," the panels "Shaker red." The "tin safe," with pierced panels for ventilation, is a Midwestern form.

Illustrations of Kentucky Shaker work from the Index of American Design, National Gallery of Art.

but of a quality of workmanship which aimed at perfection. Though Kentucky furniture and other crafts show regional variations due to period of settlement, local resources, traditions and skills of members, they are closely related to Shaker work in other parts of the country because of the unification of all colonies under the central authority at New Lebanon.

Shaker settlements had their own saw- and gristmills, blacksmiths' shops, and usually tanneries, shoemaking, and tailoring shops. A *Tailor's Division System*, published in 1849 at South Union, contains diagrams and designs to simplify and standardize the making of the brethren's clothes. A whiskey distillery was built at South Union in 1823. Pleasant Hill had hatters' and coopers' shops, and woolen, carding, fulling, and linseed-oil mills.

Shaker hands and looms produced rugs — woven, braided, and shirred — as well as bonnets and home-dyed cloth. Especially noteworthy in the Kentucky settlements were the hand and neck kerchiefs, woven in soft but luminous pinks, greens, and violets, of silk from imported silkworms.

After the Civil War a slow decline of the Shaker colonies in Kentucky began, ending in the present century with the dissolution of the Pleasant Hill colony in 1910 and of that at South Union in 1922. Today only their buildings remain, silent witnesses to an historic experiment in communal association.

RESTORATION VIEW of Pleasant Hill (Shakertown), Kentucky, as it would have looked a century ago. The four roads lead to Lexington (upper right), to the Kentucky River (lower right), to Harrodsburg (middle left), and to Danville (lower left). The stone Center Family Residence, opposite the frame Meeting House, near the junction of the Danville and Harrodsburg-Lexington Pikes, forms the focus of the town. Holy Sinai's Plain, for outdoor religious meetings, is behind the Meeting House. To the right of the Meeting House are the Minister's Dwelling and the Guest House. The large brick building across the road and to the right is the East Family Residence, balanced at the far (left) end of the road by the West Family Residence. The North Family Residence is the one farthest out the Lexington Pike. Outstanding among the other buildings were the stone Schoolhouse (nearest the Center Family Residence), and the first house erected, the little building at the head of the road leading to the river, both

destroyed. Subsidiary buildings include wash houses, weaving houses, shops, ice houses, barns, and other farm buildings and small dwellings. *Drawing by Clay Lancaster.*

The Shakers of Maine

BY MARIUS B. PÉLADEAU

A REGIONAL BIAS in all aspects of Shaker studies has caused the Shakers of Maine to be undeservedly neglected. Originally there were three Shaker Societies in the state, divided into seven "families." They were all informally started in 1782 and organized under the Shaker covenant in the following decade. The first was the Society at Alfred, with three families. Sabbathday Lake also had three families, while Gorham had only one. The Gorham group moved in 1819 to Poland Hill, near Sabbathday Lake, and closed in 1887 owing to a decline in membership. In 1931 Alfred merged with Sabbathday Lake, where the remaining Shaker sisters still live. The village today is a living museum under the direction of Dr. Theodore E. Johnson, with three of the buildings open to the public. Indeed, Sabbathday Lake is the last active Shaker community in existence.

Order and planning characterized the activities of the Shakers of Maine. At Alfred and Sabbathday Lake the buildings were aligned in three more or less parallel rows on both sides of the main road. As befitted a monastic order the brethren and sisters' Dwelling was almost directly opposite the Meetinghouse. The buildings—basically in the late Georgian and Federal styles stripped of all ornamentation—were clustered close enough so that communication was possible even in the deepest winter snow and spring mud.

In many Shaker communities the buildings appear to be placed somewhat at random, but this is not the case in Maine, where symmetrical plans were adhered to for more than a century as buildings were erected, replaced, or moved. Individual buildings were planned for maximum utility with sewing rooms, for example, facing south and west for maximum light, and laundry rooms on the main floor so that heavy loads of wet wash could be taken to the clotheslines without having to be carried up and down stairs.

The Sabbathday Lake community has some of the finest unaltered examples of Shaker architecture in the Northeast. The collection of furniture and artifacts in the museum there—with a natural emphasis on Maine pieces—is one of the most extensive anywhere, and the library houses one of the finest collections of Shaker manuscripts and documents. In 1969 the seventeen buildings and nineteen hundred acres of land that comprise the community were made a Historic District and placed on the National Register of Historic Places. This month it is also to be designated a National Historic Landmark by the Federal government.

The Meetinghouse is the keystone of any Shaker village, and the one at Sabbathday Lake, built in 1794 by Brother Moses Johnson,[1] is the finest surviving Shaker church (Fig. 1). The interior woodwork has never been repainted, and neither electricity nor a heating system has ever been installed. The entire first floor is one large room which was used for religious services (Pl. II). On the second floor are apartments and working space originally used by the Ministry Elders and Eldresses (see Pl. III), and the commodious third floor accommodated visiting ministries from other communities.

When the Ministry Elders and Eldresses outgrew their living quarters in the Meetinghouse, a new Ministry Shop was built next to the Meetinghouse in 1839 (see Fig. 1, Pl. V). Although they worked, as did all Shakers, it was stipulated that they do so separately. To the roof line the building has not been altered since its construction in 1839. In 1875 it was given a more steeply pitched roof to provide additional space on the second floor and greater storage space in the attic (Pl. IV). Behind the shop was a separate carriage shed for use by the Ministry. Just north of it was the school, built in 1880, but moved in the 1950's to a neighboring farm. It is hoped that soon it will be moved

Fig. 1. Shaker Meetinghouse of 1794 (background) and Ministry Shop of 1839 (foreground) at Sabbathday Lake, Maine. The buildings are connected by a sidewalk of large granite slabs which also once extended from the Meetinghouse across the main road to the Dwelling opposite. *Photograph by the author.*

Figs. 2, 3. Trustees' Office and Dwelling of 1816 (top foreground) at Sabbathday Lake. It has been remodeled several times. The Dwelling of 1883-1884 (top background and below) dominates the landscape of the village both because it is the only masonry building and because of its size (the main block measures forty by eighty feet). The need to complete the building quickly led the Shakers to hire outside masons to do the brickwork, but the brethren themselves quarried the large granite foundation stones from a vein of fine granite on Shaker land. Inside, twin staircases rise for five stories, one for the brethren and the other for the sisters. The main block has forty-eight bedrooms, while the wing contains a root cellar below ground, a kitchen and dining room on the first floor, and a large meeting room on the top floor. *Author's photographs.*

back to its original site and restored. South of the Meetinghouse was the Seed House, built about 1820 and taken down in 1926 (see Fig. 6) since it was a Shaker custom that once a building was no longer useful it should be removed. Another Shaker custom was that buildings could be recycled. For example, an eighteenth-century house with a hipped roof, which once stood more than a mile away from the village, was moved next to the Dwelling in the middle of the nineteenth century. There it was remodeled and used as the Brethren's Shop until it was taken down in 1916.

Across the road from the Meetinghouse and anchoring the east side of the village is the massive brick Dwelling (Figs. 2, 3) erected in 1883 and 1884 to replace the original wooden Dwelling of 1795 which had become too small for the community's needs. Although it is a late building by Shaker standards, the interior reflects the same attention to fine detail and room planning that characterizes structures erected fifty to seventy-five years earlier. The built-in cupboards, drawers, and storage chests are as chaste in design and as flawless in execution as those found on the first floor of the Ministry Shop of 1839.

South of the Dwelling is the Trustees' Office and Dwelling (Fig. 2) where the Shakers charged with conducting business with the outside world lived and operated a store for the public. It was built in 1816 as a Second House for elderly brethren and sisters and was remodeled later in the century for the Trustees. It is still operated by the Shaker sisters as a store selling Shaker-made fancy goods and other products. South of the present Trustees' Office once stood the original Trustees' Office and Dwelling which was built in 1796, later became the Hired Men's House (see Fig. 6), and was taken down in the 1950's.

North of the Dwelling stands the Girls' Shop, where girls left with the Shakers lived and studied various skills (see Fig. 4). Since the foundations have not been altered and the framing is of the period it is probably the original 1796 building, although both the interior and exterior were extensively remodeled in 1901.

The second row of buildings at Sabbathday Lake, as at other Shaker villages, is composed of workshops, barns, and other work and farm buildings. At the north end behind

Pl. I.   Bedroom in the Boys' Shop, Sabbathday Lake, Maine. The chair, tiger-maple drop-leaf table, three-tier hanger, and painted bench are all from Sabbathday Lake. The coverlets were woven by Maine Shakers; the foot locker is from Alfred, and the two beds are from the Shaker community at Mount Lebanon, New York. *Color photographs are by David Serette.*

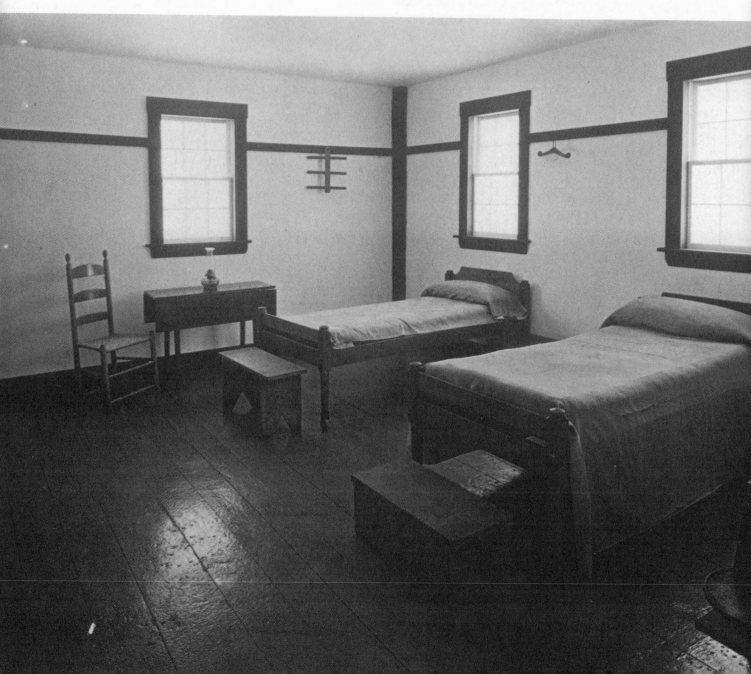

Pl. II. Meeting room on the first floor of the Meetinghouse, Sabbathday Lake. Braced and boxed beams measuring approximately eight by twenty-eight inches span the thirty-two-foot width of the building, providing the large, uncluttered floor space required by the Shakers for their religious exercises. The benches at the far end were reserved for what the Shakers called "world people" who wished to watch them worship. The pine firewood box, stained red, was made c. 1845 by Elder Joseph Brackett of Sabbathday Lake. The stove of c. 1840 is from the Mount Lebanon community.

the Girls' House is the Sisters' Shop, a cluster of buildings representing Shaker architecture between 1821 and 1910, and housing all the numerous functions performed by the sisters (see Fig. 4). Next came the Nurse House or infirmary, which was taken down in 1906, then the Herb House, erected in 1824 and today the only surviving Shaker herb house in the United States (see Fig. 5). Below it on the slope stands the Boys' Shop where boys left with the Shakers lived, went to school, and learned a trade (Pl. I and see Fig. 5). It was built in 1850 under the direction of Elder Otis Sawyer and was recently restored after a disastrous fire. Today it serves as a reception and orientation center for visitors to the Shaker Museum; there are four period rooms open to the public upstairs (see Pl. I).

Beside the Boys' Shop is the Spin House (see Fig. 5). Its large, roomy second floor was once used by the sisters for weaving and looming, although over the years other trades were practiced there too. The first floor was used to store firewood for the Trustees' Office and Dwelling directly in front of it. Next to the Spin House is a small

Fig. 4. Sisters' Shop (left), brick Dwelling and ell, and Girls' Shop and attached woodshed at Sabbathday Lake. The Sisters' Shop is a complex of buildings. The main section was built in 1821; in 1846 Deacon James Holmes' shop (built in 1812) was moved from its original location and attached to it. Various ells and additions were annexed to the shop over the years, the last one built in 1910 by Brother Delmer C. Wilson. The Sisters' Shop contains sewing, weaving, and looming rooms, a laundry, a preservatory for fruits and vegetables, a soap room, ironing rooms, and so forth. The Girls' Shop was built in 1796 and remodeled inside and out in 1901. Behind it is the herb garden from which the remaining sisters still harvest the herbs which they dry, blend, and package for sale. *Author's photograph.*

Fig. 6. Shaker village at Sabbathday Lake in two photographs taken at different seasons sometime between 1916 and 1926. The buildings, from left to right, are the Mill, which had a thirty-foot overshot wheel, the School, with woodshed and necessary attached, the Ministry carriage house, the roofs of the Girls' House and Sisters' Shop, the Ministry Shop with attached woodshed, the Meetinghouse, the Dwelling, the Seed House (taken down in 1926), the roof of the Herb House, the Cow Barn (which burned in 1955), the Boys' Shop, one end of the Spin House, the Trustees' Office and Dwelling, the Garage, the Ox Barn and the Horse Barn, and the Hired Men's House, originally the Trustees' Office and Dwelling. Sabbathday Lake is visible in the background. *Shaker Library, Sabbathday Lake; photographs by Brother Delmer C. Wilson.*

Fig. 5. Behind the Dwelling at Sabbathday Lake are the many work and service buildings which allowed the village to function as a self-contained entity. From left to right those shown are the Ox Barn and the attached Horse Barn, both built in 1847; the 1910 garage; the Spin House of 1816 with storage space for firewood on the first floor and workrooms for the sisters on the second; the Boys' Shop of 1850; and finally the Herb House of 1824, the only surviving Shaker herb house in the United States. *Author's photograph.*

Fig. 7. Brethren's Shop (background), Dwelling, and part of a barn at Poland Hill, a mile from Sabbathday Lake. The imposing Dwelling was built between 1853 and 1879 entirely of granite quarried on Shaker lands. The Shakers sold the Dwelling in 1899 and it burned in 1955. *Shaker Library; Wilson photograph.*

Fig. 8. Second Family Dwelling, Alfred, Maine. The house was originally the home of Benjamin Barnes, one of the early converts to Shakerism in Alfred. The floor plan was changed to provide for the obligatory two front entrances (the left-hand one is obscured by a tree). The Dwelling is an example of how the Shakers at the end of the eighteenth century adapted existing houses for the needs of their celibate life. The Second Family property and buildings were sold after the family closed in 1917, and the private owner pulled down all the structures about 1920. *Shaker Library.*

Fig. 9. Third, or Gathering, Family Dwelling (left) and Trustees' Office and Residence at Alfred, Maine. The massive Dwelling probably dates from the late 1790's or early 1800's; the Trustees' Office from about 1820. It is uncommon to find buildings in Maine with the entrance in the gable end facing the road. *Shaker Library.*

Pl. III. Ministry Elders' bedroom on the second floor of the Meetinghouse, Sabbathday Lake. The built-in cupboard and an identical one in the Ministry Eldresses' bedroom across the hall are the oldest examples of Shaker built-in furniture extant. Although the Meetinghouse was framed in 1794 it was not until September 1797 that the interior woodwork was completed and painted. Inside the cupboard are, from top to bottom, two oval boxes made by Maine Shakers, a tin oil-lamp filler can from Sabbathday Lake, a rare eighteenth-century wig block made by Maine Shakers, and a palm-leaf sister's bonnet from Sabbathday Lake. Hanging from a peg at the left is a mop made by the Canterbury, New Hampshire, Shakers. The graceful step stool is from Alfred. The color of the floor is original.

Pl. IV. Attic of the Ministry Shop, Sabbathday Lake. The impressive bank of drawers for clothes storage was installed in 1875 when the roof of the 1839 building was raised. The room has never been repainted. The step stool was made by the Sabbathday Lake Shakers.

Pl. V. Ministry Elders' bedroom in the Ministry Shop, Sabbathday Lake. The dry sink of c. 1795 is one of the oldest pieces at Sabbathday Lake. The excellently preserved maple and pine candlestand dates c. 1820. These pieces, the bootjack, linen splash cloth, and mirror on adjustable hanger are all from Sabbathday Lake. The rocking chair is from Alfred. The color of the floor is original to the building and was also used in many other buildings at Sabbathday Lake.

(Text continued from page 1147)

garage built in 1910 by Brother Delmer C. Wilson to house the Shakers' first car, a 1910 Seldon. It is the last building in America to have been completely erected by a Shaker brother. At the southernmost end of this row, bordering the extensive fields, is the large Horse Barn, or stable, with the equally impressive Ox Barn attached to it at the side (see Fig. 5). Both were built in 1847. There was formerly another row of farm buildings behind the barns, but they are now all gone. They included a large cow barn which burned in 1955, a hen house, greenhouse, icehouse,

25

Fig. 10. Table from Alfred; maple frame, pine top. The frame is finished with an orange-tinted varnish. The broad overhang of the one-board top, and the narrow apron which accentuates the tall, graceful legs give this table a unity of design rarely surpassed in Shaker furniture. The round box and oval carrier, both of maple, were made at Alfred. The carrier is lined with blue satin and fitted with a needlecase, emery ball, and beeswax. Height of table, 28¼; width 34; depth 21 inches. *Collection of Mr. and Mrs. Marius B. Péladeau; photograph by David Serette.*

Fig. 11. Furniture and artifacts from Sabbathday Lake. The table has a one-board pine top, maple frame, and oak legs. The drawer extends the full length of the table. Height 27½, width 36¼, depth 20¼ inches. The objects on the table are, from left to right, a pine document box painted deep blue, a small woven poplar box, a large pincushion with braided poplar edging, and an oval box made of figured maple by Brother Delmer C. Wilson, the last Shaker brother and the greatest of all Shaker boxmakers. The red-stained chair has maple legs, ash splats, and a woven tape seat. Height of chair, 39 inches. *Péladeau collection; Serette photograph.*

Fig. 12. Maple candlestand from Sabbathday Lake, 1825-1850; maple. Shaker cabinetmakers redefined and simplified worldly furniture forms. The solidity and stability of this piece contrast with the fragility of Sheraton and Hepplewhite candlestands. The top is slightly dished. Height 27; diameter of top, 22 inches. *Sabbathday Lake Shaker Village; Serette photograph.*

brooder house, and other similar buildings. Only the brick Ash House behind the Sisters' Shop is left to remind us of the multitude of buildings that once made a Shaker village a complete, self-supporting agrarian community.

Not very much remains of the other Shaker villages in Maine. At Alfred, some of the buildings formerly used by the Church Family now serve as a school and monastery for a Catholic order. However, the buildings occupied by the Second (Fig. 8) and North families at Alfred are gone.

In 1808 some members of the North Family moved from Alfred to Gorham, Maine, to augment the small Society there. Their large Dwelling, built in that year, is still one of the highlights of Maine Shaker architecture. Its exterior is that of a typical, large-scale, square New England house and illustrates how the Shakers used styles of building common to the region they lived in, and merely adapted the interiors to the needs of their celibate life. The Gorham dwelling still retains its splendid double stair which starts as one and then divides halfway to the second floor so that the brethren and sisters could enter the second-floor meeting room for religious services through separate doors. A number of other Shaker buildings at Gorham—probably shops and secondary dwellings—still survive in private hands.

In 1819 the Gorham Shakers moved to the top of Poland Hill, a mile north of Sabbathday Lake. In 1853 they began to build a huge granite Dwelling there (Fig. 7), but financial difficulties delayed its completion until 1879. Declining membership forced this family to merge with the Sabbathday Lake community in 1887 and the Poland Hill property

26

Fig. 13. Night stand from Alfred, c. 1840; pine. The turnings at the bottom of the legs are often found on non-Shaker Maine furniture of the period and demonstrate that the Shakers were always observing the world around them and borrowing the features that fitted their concept of design. Height 27, width 26¾, depth 19¾ inches. *Sabbathday Lake Village; Serette photograph.*

Fig. 14. Maple bed, probably from Alfred. Beds made by the Maine Shakers are uncommon today and this is the finest known example. The sleeping area measures four by six feet and was probably used by two boys or girls. It is hinged near the head so that it could be folded up against the wall. Height of headboard, 36; width 54; length 78 inches. *Private collection; Serette photograph.*

Fig. 14a. Detail of the bed shown in Fig. 14. The excellence of the turnings and hinge construction are evident. Note the close relationship between the legs on this bed and those on the table from Alfred shown in Fig. 10.

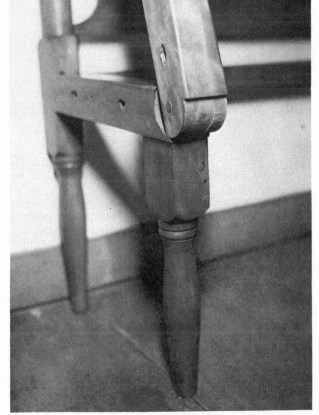

was sold to private interests in 1899. The buildings there burned or were torn down in the 1950's.

Like the architecture, the furniture made by the Maine Shakers is more individualistic and forceful than that of communities outside the state (Figs. 10-14). While New York and Massachusetts Shaker pieces often appear to have been stamped from a single mold, Maine Shaker furniture reflects a less rigid tradition in which men of talent were better able to express their inventiveness.[2] Even the colors used by the Maine Shakers are bolder and brighter than those used elsewhere. It is as though they recognized that design never stands still, but must always change if it is to remain valid and meaningful.

The Maine Shakers worked long and hard to wrest a living from an unyielding soil, but theirs was a life motivated by religion so that far from being dour and humorless, as Maine Yankees are reputed to be, they were alive, vibrant, and inventive. These qualities are reflected in their architecture, furniture, and way of life as a whole.

[1]For an article about the meetinghouses of Moses Johnson see ANTIQUES for October 1970, pp. 594-599.

[2]For an article about the furniture made by Elder Henry Green of Alfred, Maine, see ANTIQUES for May 1974, pp. 1119-1125.

SHAKER INSPIRATIONAL DRAWINGS

By EDWARD D. ANDREWS

EVER SINCE that time in Manchester, England, about 1772, when the Lord Jesus appeared to the imprisoned Ann Lee, the mill girl and prophetess who became the first leader of the Shaker sect, the "Shaking Quakers," or Believers in Christ's Second Appearing, have been visionists and mystics. The reality of spiritual presences was re-demonstrated when, after Ann's release, a mysterious power protected her and her followers from the clubs and stones of their Lancashire persecutors, and again when she was enabled to confound her accusers by speaking in unknown tongues. Shortly before the little band, seeking freedom of worship, embarked for America in 1774, James Whittaker, Ann's chief disciple, had a vision of the new country, and "saw a large tree, and every leaf thereof shone with such brightness, as made it appear like a burning torch, representing the Church of Christ, which will yet be established in this land" (*Fig. 3*). On the ship Mariah, during a severe storm, two angels were seen standing by the mast assuring the passengers of a safe arrival in the new world; and the first religious dances were learned from visions of angels dancing around the throne of God.

As the Shaker movement spread through New York and

HUNDREDS of the Shaker drawings here discussed — no one knows how many — once existed in the eighteen main branches of the United Society of Believers. Most of those here illustrated, with others, chiefly from New Lebanon, New York, and Hancock, Massachusetts, are in the author's collection. About eighty-five have been documented. The present article is based on an unpublished monograph.

agency. Leaders were chosen, and their authority sanctioned, by divine revelation. The statutes governing the organization and administration of church order were inspired laws. Visions abounded. In the rapture of sensing the imminence of the holy spirit, diverse "gifts" were received by young and old, and songs and rituals found their strange origin.

Some fifty years after the establishment of the United Society a great revival — known as "Mother Ann's Work," or "Ann's Second Appearing" — broke out among the Shakers, during which such gifts flowered in many remarkable forms. In the spring of 1838, about eight months after the first "manifestations" at the Niskeyuna (New York) colony, messages from the spirit of the prophetess were received at New Lebanon, in the same state, through the medium of chosen "instruments." Speaking in the name of their heavenly parent, these inspired visionists called upon the Believers, in meeting, to return to the true order of the church, to purge out disorders and superfluities, to confess their sins, to mortify the flesh by bowing, reeling, shaking, and kissing one another's feet. It was not long before similar ceremonies were observed in the other seventeen societies. Blessings were bestowed on young and old. Spiritual wine was dispensed "which carried a great evidence of its reality, by the paroxysms of intoxication which it produced, causing those who drank it to stagger and reel, like drunken people." A particular phenomenon was the distribution of spiritual presents, symbolic of the virtues of the Shaker life but bearing the names of material things: gold leaf, books, musical instruments, fruits and flowers, diamonds, numerous articles of ornament, boxes and baskets, implements of hand labor, weapons of war, and sacks full of all kinds of rich treasures. From the instruments, as well as from others subject to the mysterious influences of the revival, proceeded a stream of messages — prophecies, warnings and exhortations — many new dance forms,

New England, and after the turn of the century into Kentucky, Ohio, and Indiana, the tenets of the faith — celibacy and purity of mind, separation from worldliness and the world, confession of sin, community of goods or "joint interest"—continued to find support and validity through supernatural

and hundreds of "gift" or "vision" tunes and songs.

Action was pantomimic, gestures may sometimes have been grotesque, but the emotions which accompanied the bestowal and acceptance of gifts were genuine. When presents or communications were received by the Believers from their "heavenly parents" (Christ and Mother Ann), their "spiritual parents" (Father Joseph Meacham, the American-born organizer of the order; Mother Lucy Wright, his successor as head of the church; Father William Lee, Ann's brother; Father James Whittaker; and other early leaders or biblical prophets), and finally, from their "eternal parents," Almighty God and Holy Mother Wisdom

FIG. 1 (*above*) — SACRED SHEET. Sent from Holy Mother Wisdom, by her Holy Angel of many signs, for Sister Adah Zillah Potter. Received March 5, 1843. Written March 22, 1843. In the first Order on the Holy Mount (New Lebanon). Instruments, Semantha Fairbanks and Mary Wicks. Design in black ink on white paper, 8 by 13 inches.

FIG. 2 (*right*) — HEART GIFT OR REWARD. The Word of the Holy Heavenly Father. To a child of his Delight, James Goodwin. Inscriptions on both sides, and symbols on one side of white paper. Pen and ink. New Lebanon, 1844.

— the illusion in the Shaker mind was absolute and highly dramatic.

For several years the manifestations were ritualistic, behavioristic, spontaneous. In 1840 scribes were chosen to record, in beautifully written hymnals and journals, the songs, testimonies, and messages, but no attempt was made to picture the mystic experiences of the revival until about 1845, when the afflatus itself was beginning to subside. True, Mary Hazzard, an eldress at the church family in New Lebanon, had "pricked"· one of her lovely songs around the border of a leaf design in a hymnal dated 1839. Cryptic "sacred sheets" symbolizing the orderly beauty of heaven (*Fig. 1*) appeared in 1843. The leaf "rewards" — delicately inscribed green paper cutouts representing leaves from the tree of life — were first exchanged in the period 1843-1844, and the pink, yellow or white paper hearts (*Fig. 2*) — where decorative devices such as angels, crowns, swords, doves, and the like make their initial appearance — in 1844. But these tokens of love and merit, in a sense, were tentative forerunners of those designs in which the artist's imagination, hitherto suppressed by prohibitions on all display and ornament, was fully released. The major drawings, covering the years from 1845 to 1859, seem indeed the expression of "emotions recollected in tranquillity," the "remembrance of things past," recalling Proust's contention that there is nothing significant in any occurrence until it is remembered.

These later inspirationals fall into two general groups, not too distinct: those depicting

simple floral and arboreal designs and emblems, variously interpreted, usually done in color, with the Tree of Life as a favorite device; and those in which the symbolism is more elaborate and abstract. Floral motifs and plant forms persist in the latter, but do not dominate a carefully planned and often detailed pattern rich with allegorical meanings; some are in color, while others are delicately rendered with a pen in blue, or blue and red inks. There are also two main, though sometimes merging, sources of inspiration: the beauty of nature, as represented in fruits and flowers, arbors, leaves, trees, plants, gardens, fountains, rivers, precious stones, the sun, moon, and stars; and the Scriptures, especially the books of Genesis, Esdras, and Revelation. As to the first, the mystic communion of the Believers with God involved a sensitive kinship with nature, a love of color and form subtly revealed in many ways and now openly expressed. They had built their communities in beautiful places, had "redeemed" the soil with affection, had cultivated plants and flowers for the health of body and spirit. Perhaps, before they had become Shakers, they were familiar with the floral patterns on appliqué or embroidered quilts, hooked rugs, samplers, wall papers, needlepoint, or stencils. Perhaps they adapted their designs from biblical allusions. Whatever the source, the limners turned to the beauty surrounding them for the fittest expression of a perfect immortal world. That the Scriptures furnished an equally rich field of images is

apparent from the emblems and legends in many, especially the more complex drawings: the well of Samaria, the ark, "the cup from which the Saviour drank at the well," Abram's altar, the Red Sea, "Sarah of old," Jephtha, the woman of Samaria, shew-bread, and so on. The wine press and vineyard, angels, doves, trumpets, harps, and fountains (a symbol, with the ancient Hebrews, of life-giving power and celestial happiness) were favorite subjects. The sickle, the lamps and candlesticks, the seals, the golden chariots, the pillar of light, "the moon turned to blood," the chart of the heavenly Jerusalem, the cross, the all-seeing eye, the lamb and dove, the bread plant, the fig and weeping willow trees, the Cedar of Paradise, the bower of mulberry trees, may all be traced to the same origin.

However, the meanings ascribed to such emblems were seldom stereotyped. A tree may be

The Tree of Life, all pure and clean
Of God the Fathers planting;
On Zions hill, it firm doth stand,
And well establish'd, by God's hand.
Not like the house, upon the sand,
But firm by heaven's granting.

But it also may represent a celestial plum tree, a cedar of paradise, the "cherry tree brought from spiritual England," a tree bearing manna or "strange fruits," "the gospel union, fruit bearing tree," or a tree of light, comfort, order, virtue, or protection. Similarly, a rose may signify love or chastity, though sometimes it may typify patience, perseverance, or faith. As in the spiritual "gifts" exchanged in meeting, there were balls of light, love, and union; diamonds of peace and comfort; chains of strength and union; boxes or baskets of treasures.

Objects precious and rare in a worldly sense — golden chains, crowns, ornaments, and exotic flowers and foods — served more literally to suggest the wonders and joys of a supernatural world. And when clocks or watches, angels with protective wings outspread, or "a ship of safety," are used the intent is obvious. Yet there was, on the whole, considerable freedom and individuality of expression. Not only in the ascription of emblems, but in the decorative borders of some of the

FIG. 6 (left) — FLORAL WREATH. From Father James, Father Joseph, Mother Lucy and Mother Dana for the Ministry at the City of Peace (Hancock), December 4, 1853. Design in colors. 12 inches square.

drawings, the free use of color, and the explanatory legends and inscriptions, there is evidence of original and versatile talent. The period in which the drawings were composed was too brief, indeed, to produce a "school."

Most if not all of the inspirationals were done by sisters of the order, though some were dedicated to, and perhaps actually presented to beloved brethren and sisters, to elders and eldresses, and especially to the Ministry or "lead." Apparently the heart, leaf, fan and seal tokens were freely exchanged, but the larger designs, if employed as gifts, were — in accord with the code against ornament and individual privilege — never displayed.

In fact, we cannot be sure whether there was a clear purpose behind their creation. The only allusion in Shaker literature is the following passage in Isaac Young's manuscript history (1857): "There have been many notices to individuals this year past [1843] . . . with many drawings, signs, and figures of objects in the spirit world, with mysterious writings, etc. which will, it is said, at some future time be revealed and explained."

There is a Shaker tradition that the writings and drawings were sometimes automatically controlled or "dictated by a spirit," and in at least one example, a tree design by Hannah Cohoon of Hancock (Fig. 7) — notable because the signature appears on the work — the artist testifies that its identity was revealed to her

FIG. 7 (center) — TREE OF LIFE. Design in colors. City of Peace (Hancock), July 3, 1854. Seen and painted by Hannah Cohoon. Size of drawing, 18 by 23 inches.

FIG. 8 (left) — AN EMBLEM OF THE HEAVENLY SPHERE. A Gift from Mother Ann, Given January, 1854. Dictated by the Prophetess Deborah. (Judg. iv) Hancock community. Design in colors, 19 by 24 inches. Forty-eight "saints in order" are represented, beginning with Mother Ann, Father William, and the Savior, and including biblical figures and Christopher Columbus.

by Mother Ann's moving the hand of a medium "to write twice over, Your Tree is the Tree of Life." The inspirationals were the product of a profoundly moving experience and it may be argued that the forces of spiritualism unlocked the doors of the subconscious Shaker mind, sanctioning an open expression of human desires and the vicarious enjoyment of the same. Unused to games or recreation, the Believers tossed to one another glistening "spheres of love." Opposed to instrumental music, they listened with rapture to spiritual harps, to shining trumpets, to the "holy musical instrument of God" with its "fifteen connecting instruments." Intolerant of jewelry, they imagined themselves adorned with chains of pure gold, with diamonds, pearls, amethysts, and sapphires, with golden finger rings and costly gems. Living in plain dwellings, they envisaged the ornamental structures of heaven. Used to the simplest food, they relished the "sweet scented manna" and the exotic fruits of the tree of life. Long accustomed to utensils of pewter, wood, and stoneware, they found satisfaction, during their symbolic sacraments, in drinking from silver cups and eating from golden bowls. Denying the state and refusing to bear arms, they thrilled to the waving of flags, and buckled upon themselves swords, breastplates, and spiritual armor. On sheets of gold and on rolls in radiant colors were the heavenly messages delivered. Humbly laboring without wage or material reward, the Believers welcomed the mantles, crowns, and wreaths spiritually bestowed, the golden sacks of comfort, the golden chariots ready to take them to their eternal home. Was it not as a compensation for their own plain apparel that the Shakers, before marching to their hill-top festivals, joyfully clothed themselves in the garments of the blessed?

Though an element of compensation may have entered into the content, the control of form and precision of execution (involving in some instances the aid of a compass, ruled lines, and preliminary sketches) are evidence of deliberate creation, far removed from the crude scrawls and indeterminate pictures accepted as automatic. The "vision" of the instrument was not immediately committed to paper,

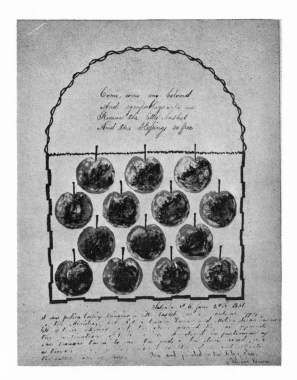

FIG. 9 — FRUIT DESIGN. "Seen and painted in the City of Peace [Hancock] by Hannah Cohoon." Inscription: "I saw Judith Collins bringing a little basket full of beautiful apples for the Ministry, from Brother Calvin Harlow and Mother Sarah Harrison. It is their blessing and the chain around the bail represents the combination of their blessing. I noticed in particular as she brought them to me the ends of the stems looked fresh as though they were just picked by the stems and set into the basket one by one." (Brother Calvin and Mother Sarah were the first "lead" at Hancock.) In colors. Date, 1856.

FIG. 10 (below) — TREE OF COMFORT. "A Gift from Mother Ann, August, 1859, to Eldress Eunice [Hastings], with the Heavenly Fr. and holy Mother's blessing." Design in colors. Hancock.

nor always drawn by the one who had the vision or idea. Though the Shakers themselves have been noncommittal, and in some cases have repudiated the testimonies of the period and disposed of the drawings, there is evidence that those members of the order with a natural talent for drawing and penmanship were encouraged to render in graphic form, as a means of promoting the afflatus, the experiences which were common to the whole membership. Like the songs and dances, the messages from the instruments and other gifts, they thus served an educative purpose. This view receives confirmation in an account of a mountain meeting in which the Savior, speaking through an instrument, declares: "I would instruct those that do not clearly understand the work of God, by means and ways that ye may understand, comparing heavenly and divine things to the similitudes of earth." And again, in one of the remarkable books published at the time, the author, Philemon Stewart, writes: "All the presents . . . have been sent forth in this degree or nearness and semblance of material things that do exist on earth, that you might be better able to appreciate in lively colors, and thrilling sensations, the real adornings and beauties of the spiritual world, or the abodes of the righteous, in the paradise of God."

However, if such were the purpose of the drawings, probably not all of them were thus employed. With the possible exception of the small gifts, they received little publicity; few Believers at the time, or since, knew of their existence. That they were sanctioned by the ruling order, the ministry, is obvious; but in retrospect they seem neither automatic nor didactic expressions, but rather purely creative compositions produced by selected individuals as a reaction to an experience which was personal, but which at the same time reflected the spiritual outlook of the whole community. As such the drawings should properly be considered a religious and a true folk art.

In the preface to a book which contains an account of the manifestations at Canterbury, New Hampshire, the Shaker author found it fitting to quote the following lines from Lamartine:
Beauty's the form of things unseen,
Save to the soul's desire.

The Coming Shaker Exhibition in Manhattan

A Gallery Note

THE exhibition of Shaker furniture to be held at the Whitney Museum in New York from November 12 to December 15 should attract wide attention. Those collectors of things antique who are particularly fond of the simple, homely, handmade things of earlier days will quite naturally admire the seeming naïveté of Shaker products. A few other folk will look deeper to perceive in the unadorned placidity of these objects a tangible revelation of the tranquil spirit that may accompany profound religious faith.

I shall be particularly interested to observe the reactions of the modernistic tribe. The sole purpose of Shaker furniture was to serve particular utilitarian needs. Each piece was designed with reference to function and function only, and with a conscious and careful avoidance of ornamental features. Hence as a whole this furniture comports, in theory at least, with the ideas of sundry contemporary designers. Furthermore, many of its visible features will at least faintly remind the observer of latter-day creations in the domain of domestic equipment. Yet between the prototypical functionalism of Shakerdom and the modern brand spreads an immeasurable gulf: for, after all, the one, despite its shell of stark impersonality, is yet to the sensitive eye aureate with warm human emotion, perhaps the more potent because infinitely pure; of the other, no superficial smartness of line or sophistication of finish can long mask the essential

Fig. 1 — INSPIRATIONAL DRAWING *(1849)*
Probably by Eldress Polly Reed of the New Lebanon, New York, community. In colors on pale blue paper. *Size,* 14 by 16 ½ inches.
This and other illustrations from the collection of Mr. and Mrs. Edward D. Andrews

Fig. 2 — INSPIRATIONAL DRAWING *(1848)*
Ascribed to Eldress Polly Reed. These drawings were not for wall display, but were personal offerings appropriately cherished. *Size,* 14 by 14 ½ inches

artificiality or compensate for the chill aloofness that invariably overspreads the spiritually untenanted.

But to return to the exhibition. Here for the first time will be shown a number of pictures that reveal a hitherto almost unknown and unrecognized phase of Shaker life and activity. These are the so-called inspirational drawings, dating for the most part from the 1840's and 1850's, when, it would appear, the sect was responsive to influences that may perhaps be characterized as occult. During this period were held ceremonies that could hardly have been seriously enacted except by participants elevated to ecstasy by some form of hypnosis. Such group upliftings were reflected in individual experience. Superterrestrial voices spoke messages to ears attuned to ethereal vibrations, and holy symbols were disclosed to eyes aware of the unseen. The urge to capture such symbols and record their forms and meanings for the benefit of the faithful became so strong as to overcome the prevailing injunctions against pictorial representation of any kind.

As a result we find a considerable group of drawings, some executed simply in line with pen and a bluish ink, others brilliant with clear and shining colors: blues, bright pinks, a lambent yellow, and lively greens. The tints employed are in general much cleaner than those encountered in Pennsylvania *fractur* work or in the illuminated genealogies of New England. Their delicacy and unsullied sweetness suggest that, like Fra Angelico, the Shaker artists were striving to emulate the immaculate and lovely hues of heaven.

In respect both to color and to the fundamentals of

technique, the Shaker inspirational drawings are obviously unrelated to the so-called primitive designs produced outside the precincts of Shaker communities. In their arrangement and in the stylizing of their symbols, however, they develop methods and achieve effects that many superficial observers assume to have been derived from Pennsylvania illuminations. With such a judgment I am in complete disagreement. The Shaker fashion of more or less symmetrically balancing elements on each side of a middle line is an almost unconscious and inevitable procedure. The variety obtained within this simple unity may possibly be credited to dim recollections of old sampler patterns. Some of the motives are quite literal renderings of familiar objects, some are simplifications of natural forms expressed in terms virtually universal in folk or primitive art. For others it seems impossible to account except by some theory of automatism. By a like theory must we explain the extreme neatness and deftness of workmanship that distinguishes these strangely fascinating portrayals. We may not, of course, deny that their authors were possessed of native artistic talent, perhaps of inherited memories stirred to life by emotional excitement. But that a gift long denied release should at one leap reach so high a level of decorative and technical mastery as we discover in these drawings becomes comprehensible only when we accept some part of the doctrine of inspiration.

In these brief notes I may not even attempt to analyze Shaker drawings in detail or to interpret their symbolism. I shall have fulfilled my intention if I convince my readers that these works of art are worthy of study as independent phenomena, whose resemblance to other primitive creations is not due to any process of imitation but instead is the evidence of a kinship of the subconscious so deeply and universally implanted in humankind as to be almost unaffected either by differences of physical circumstances or by discrepancies of time.   — H. E. K.

Fig. 3 — INSPIRATIONAL DRAWING (*1847*)
In pen and ink without added coloring. Note the "heavenly trumpet," the "heavenly lamp" — apparently of the lard-oil type, the "musical instrument," and the dove bearing a branch from the tree of the Holy Mother. Circular sheet slightly reduced from the original size

II Architecture

Although almost everyone today is drawn to admire the clean lines of Shaker architecture, this was not always so. In the Victorian era the great buildings, constructed to house the brothers and sisters, were felt to be plain to the point of austerity. The Victorians, most certainly, never entertained the notion of these buildings as "beautiful." Today, however, we derive a sense of harmony from this strong, plain style, and we admire the perfection of workmanship of its parts. The Shakers turned to daily prayer for spiritual guidance. They were inspired to follow many unique ideas which gave them a reputation for inventiveness. This, coupled with functionalism and the lack of any applied decorative embellishments, produced a truly original style easily identified as Shaker whether it be the round barn at Hancock, Massachusetts, or the prayer-like rise of the twin spiral stairways in the Trustees' House at Pleasant Hill, Kentucky. In this section on architecture two of the many famous builders of the period are discussed, but there were many more just as dedicated who remained anonymous.

The following quotations from Mother Ann Lee are all too familiar, and yet they explain the depth of the Shaker devotion to balance and harmony:

> Labor to make the way of God your own; let it be your inheritance, your treasure, your occupation, your daily calling.

> Do all your work as though you had a thousand years to live, and as you would if you knew you must die tomorrow.

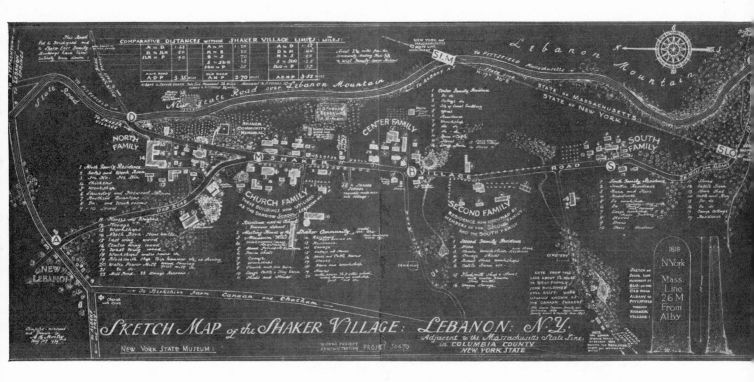

SKETCH MAP of the SHAKER VILLAGE: LEBANON. N.Y.
Adjacent to the Massachusetts State Line
in COLUMBIA COUNTY
NEW YORK STATE

The architecture of the Shakers

BY D. M. C. HOPPING AND GERALD R. WATLAND

THE KEY TO THE ARCHITECTURE of the Shakers lies in their creed. Simplicity, honesty, lack of ornamentation are as much characteristics of their buildings as of the Believers themselves. This is an early example of functional form in the architecture of this country: their withdrawal from the world, their consecration of themselves and their property to God, the holding of their goods in common, their belief in a celibate life, their respect for work, all affected what the Shakers built. Among the early converts were carpenter-builders of considerable ability, who helped set the pattern of building that was followed in subsequent communities. Painstaking workmanship and a sense of order shine out in every structure, no matter of what size or importance. In style, all the buildings evolved from the simple types common in the New England countryside at the period. The earliest were of wood, and, except for the church, which was white, were painted a straw color with deep-red shingle roofs. As the Shakers prospered and gained in members, masonry materials were used. Fine granite and marble-faced stone foundations are found below four-storied brick buildings in many communities. Paths between the buildings were paved with huge flat stones.

Except for variations dictated by distinctive features of the landscape, all the communities were similar both in their architecture and in the pattern of assemblage of their buildings. This was chiefly because all groups were governed by the same ideals and rigid regulations, but also because of collaboration among the various "families" in their building enterprises. Periodic visits to the communities by the governing body of the central ministry also kept them in conformity.

The meetinghouses were reduced to the simplest form possible. Two private entrances were provided for the male and female clergy, at one end of a simple rectangle. Separate entrances for the brethren and sisters were on the long side of the building. All entrances gave on a large plain room, unobstructed except for a few rows of seats along one side for the use of visitors. To obtain this unobstructed floor space, a huge truss was necessary to support the roof. At New Lebanon, the Shakers' ingenuity was shown in the design of an arched type known in the architectural profession as a "rainbow roof." This form was repeated in the hoods over the doorways. White paint was reserved for use on the exteriors of the meetinghouses according to the Millennial Laws recorded at New Lebanon in 1821.

The residence buildings were invariably multi-storied, whether of wood or masonry construction. Two separate entrances were provided for the two sexes and generally the entrances were hooded. The elders occupied separate apartments on the main floor, with brethren and sisters living, dormitory-style, in the rooms above. Though several brethren or several sisters occupied each room, only one small cupboard with shelves was provided, as the Shakers had no possessions of their own. Wood peg

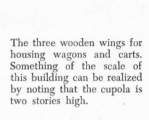

The three wooden wings for housing wagons and carts. Something of the scale of this building can be realized by noting that the cupola is two stories high.

The great stone barn of the North family at New Lebanon.

Skeleton section sketch
of stone barn,
North family, New Lebanon.

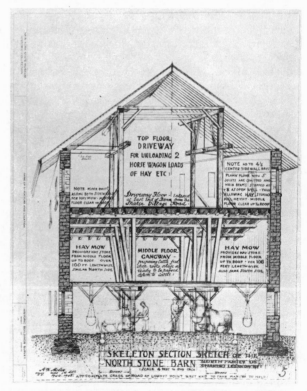

rails were built in on all four walls for the hanging of garments, hats, chairs, baskets. The Shakers were clever in locating their chimneys: nearly every room had an outlet for a small cast-iron stove of distinctive character, made according to the Shakers' own design. Often the basements of the residence buildings were put to use as laundries, kitchens, or shops.

The dominant building in each community was the barn, whether of stone or wood. Since the Shaker economy was largely agricultural, the barns were invariably huge. That of the North family at New Lebanon, pictured here, was 296 feet long, fifty feet wide, and five stories high! As in several other communities, it was built into the hillside, in order to provide access for unloading on all levels. The upper floors were used for storage of hay and grain. Below, on the main grade level, the cows were kept. At one end was a tremendous manure pit, filled by a system of buckets run around on a semicircular catwalk at the main level where the cows were, and emptied at the level below. In instances where the barn was on level ground, this same accessibility of all floors was achieved by building a series of ramps. In conjunction with the great barns, wooden wings were constructed to house wagons and carts. A place for everything and everything in its place was part of the Shaker creed.

While the basic activity among the Shakers was agri-

Ironing room in the laundry building of the North family at New Lebanon, showing early dryer, sink, and stove for heating flatirons.

Built-in cupboard and drawers and Shaker-designed stove in the meeting room of the main residence building at Hancock.

Meetinghouse with rainbow roof, erected 1822-1824. Church family, New Lebanon. Now a part of the Darrow school.

Maple stair railing, typical of the delicate yet sturdy craftsmanship of the Shaker carpenters.

Circular stone barn at Hancock, Massachusetts, built in 1826.

culture, many trades were practiced. Each new convert was given a job commensurate with his ability. Blacksmithing was a trade in which they excelled. All the rough and finish hardware, iron railings, nails, horseshoes, wagon wheels, and other ironwork needed for their buildings and work were manufactured in the smithies, such as the one pictured here. This small stone building of 1846, which is far superior to the usual smithy of the period, was as nearly fireproof as the Shakers could make it. Much care and craftsmanship went into its dressed-stone corners, lintels, and sills, and its typically Shaker plaster cove at the eaves. Here again is Shaker inventiveness in the flues of the chimney, all joining together below the roof line to become one above the roof. The harnessing of water power whenever feasible was another Shaker accomplishment.

The Shakers' many other pursuits required space adapted to specific purposes that ranged from weaving and dyeing cloth to sorting, packaging, and labeling garden seeds. At the South family in New Lebanon, a great barn was given over to chairmaking, one of the most important crafts. In general, however, all these operations took place in buildings nearly identical in size and style to the residence buildings, except that they were more often of wood construction than of masonry.

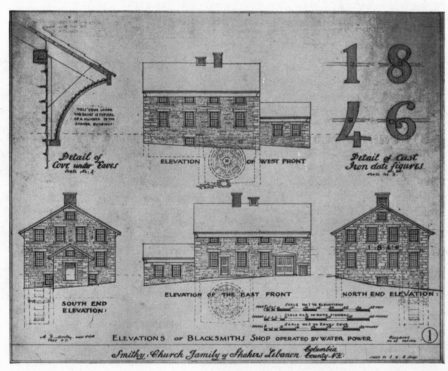

Elevations, section, and second-floor plan of blacksmith shop at New Lebanon, 1846.

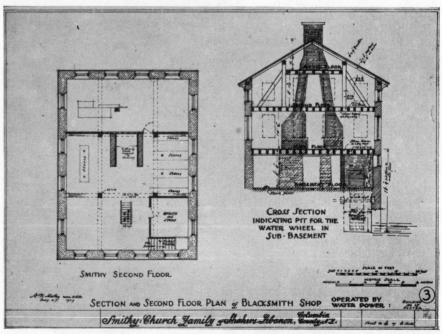

Brick buildings at
the South Union community
near Auburn, Kentucky,
established 1811.
Photograph by Clay Lancaster.

Façade of Center family residence at
Pleasant Hill, Kentucky, established
1814. Note the stone masonry, two
entrance doors, iron railings, double-
hung window sash. *Photograph by
Clay Lancaster.*

The interiors of the Shaker buildings were no less finished than the exteriors. As laid down in the Millennial Laws, definite restrictions guided the general character. "Beadings, mouldings, and cornices which are merely for fancy may not be made by the Believers." This guaranteed the architectural simplicity and severity which, in conjunction with furniture of Shaker design, are most appealing. The colors and finishes of the woodwork were also rigidly specified. "Floors in dwelling houses, if stained at all, should be of a reddish yellow, and shop floors should be of a yellowish red." The laws went on to designate that "varnish, if used in dwelling houses, may be used only to the moveables therein, as the following, viz., Tables, stands, etc. . . . no ceilings, casings or mouldings may be varnished"; however, "bannisters or handrails in dwelling houses may be varnished."

A distinguishing feature of the Shaker interior was the extensive use of built-in cupboards and drawers, in rooms other than their retiring rooms. Everywhere the inevitable peg rails surrounded the room, their wood pegs threaded so that they could be screwed into the rail. The double-hung window sashes were held in place by a trim board secured by wooden thumb screws, to facilitate the removal of the sash for washing. This as well as anything demonstrates not only the cleanliness of the Shakers but also their ingenuity.

Today these distinctive buildings have been vacated by the Shakers in all but the three still-active communities. Those at North Union, Ohio, and West Union, Indiana, have disappeared entirely, but many of the others still stand, in varying states of repair. Some are unused, some privately owned, some converted to use as schools, state institutions, and the like. They are well worth seeing; they ought to be preserved.

Both Mr. Hopping and Mr. Watland are members of the Society of Architectural Historians and active in architectural restoration work.

A Shaker house in Canaan, New York

BY EDWARD DEMING ANDREWS, *Curator, Shaker Community, Inc.*

The house was originally the sisters' shop of the Canaan (New York) Upper family of Shakers. The hooded doorway is a distinguishing feature of Shaker architecture. Sliding doors, painted a warm yellow-brown, close off the entry to provide protection in inclement weather. To the north is a flagstone terrace, a sunken garden whose walls and brick arches once formed the foundation of the family dwelling, and beyond this a young apple orchard. To the east are open fields reaching up to mountain woodland. *All photographs by William H. Tague.*

IN DECEMBER 1813 eleven Shakers gathered at Canaan, in eastern New York State, on what was called the Patterson farm, situated about two miles from the North or Novitiate family of the central Shaker community in New Lebanon. The year following they moved to the Mill House, near a gristmill a half mile from that family; then seven years later, on May 9, 1821, they moved again to another farm, the so-called Peabody Place, where the colony, now numbering thirteen brethren and fourteen sisters, formed what came to be known as the Canaan Upper family. Here, in a clearing in a fold of the Taconic Mountains, they developed a largely self-sufficient religious order, chiefly agricultural but with a number of shops for industries based on the soil.

After this secluded little community of believers closed in 1897, the buildings stood unoccupied for a number of years. The property was eventually purchased by Laura Langford, well-known feminist, author, and one of the

editors of the *Brooklyn Eagle*, whose interest in Shaker principles had been stimulated by an intimate correspondence with Eldress Anna White of the New Lebanon North family. In 1931, after Mrs. Langford's death, the property was bought by Mr. and Mrs. John Roberts, also of Brooklyn, who made it their summer home. Though some of the buildings, including the family dwelling, were by that time in bad condition, two of them—the sisters' shop, built in 1854, and another frame structure—were restored for the use of the owners and a caretaker. An 1842 barn and a wagon shed were also preserved, and the foundations of the razed buildings converted into flower, herb, and vegetable gardens.

Restoration of the sisters' shop was carried out, over a number of years, by Mr. Roberts and the late Mrs. Roberts. Being near the New Lebanon community, they found guidance, as well as furnishings, in the still existent families there, not only the North (of which the Canaan

A bell in an inner entry is rung by pulling a cord in the outer entry.

A partition was removed to give length to the living room, which is 17 feet wide and 34 feet long. The pine and maple table (14 feet long, 34 inches wide, and 27 inches high) came from a South family, New Lebanon, shop. No pictures were ever hung on Shaker walls. The carpet is home woven.

Besides the removal of a partition, the only other structural change was the installation of a 7½-foot-wide fireplace to replace the small box stoves of Shaker usage. Paneled cupboards, built into the wall above it, harmonize with the rest of the woodwork. The rocking chairs are "cushioned" with tape seats, and one has a tape back.

Mrs. Roberts' favorite armchair, with the colorful tape seat characteristic of Shaker manufacture. The simple, clean lines of the candlestand are also typically Shaker. Both pieces came from New Lebanon. To insure a free circulation of air in Shaker houses, holes (in the form of pyramids) were often bored into the baseboards. In the Roberts house, apertures above the interior doors, with delicately shaped swinging panels set into them, serve the same function.

Shakers had once been a branch) but also the Church, Second, and South families. Eldress Sarah Collins of the South family took a particular interest in the project, and from her Mr. and Mrs. Roberts obtained braided and woven rugs and many fine pieces of furniture.

Restoration was carried out with restraint and exquisite taste. Shaker furnishings were selected with discrimination. The pine floors, door and window frames, pegboards, built-in drawers and cupboards, and other woodwork were carefully cleaned down and waxed to a soft brown sheen. Most important of all, the true Shaker spirit—the gift of order and simplicity—imbues the rooms with a quiet grace. Since there is nothing superfluous or useless in them, the warm-toned furniture, the rugs and runners, the draperies, the paneling above the fireplace, the books—all show to best advantage. Spacious and bathed in light, the rooms are colorful yet serene, a happy abiding place nestling in the hills.

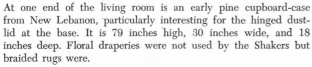

At one end of the living room is an early pine cupboard-case from New Lebanon, particularly interesting for the hinged dust-lid at the base. It is 79 inches high, 30 inches wide, and 18 inches deep. Floral draperies were not used by the Shakers but braided rugs were.

In the earliest Shaker houses and shops, drawers and cupboards were built into the walls as a means of saving space and promoting order and convenience. This pine unit, in the dining room, is 43 inches wide and a little over 8 feet high, the height of the room. Pegboards high on the wall served a similar purpose. The drop-leaf table is an early New Lebanon piece.

The Shaker meetinghouses of Moses Johnson

BY MARIUS B. PÉLADEAU

THE RELIGION OF the Shakers was centered in their devotional services, highlighted by community dancing and singing and nearly always attended by the ritualistic "shaking" dances and marches which gave the sect its name. These services were conducted in a meetinghouse, or church. In ten of the earliest Shaker communities in New England and eastern New York, the meetinghouses were of a distinctive style, with common characteristics and features. All ten of these outstanding structures were designed, framed, and built by one amazing Shaker brother, Moses Johnson. As the first Shaker builder whose work can be documented, Johnson may be said to have formed the style of Shaker architecture.

The Shaker meetinghouses which can be credited to Moses Johnson are, in chronological order: Mount Lebanon, New York; Hancock, Massachusetts; Watervliet, New York; Enfield, Connecticut; Harvard, Massachusetts; Canterbury, New Hampshire; Shirley, Massachusetts; Enfield, New Hampshire; and Alfred and Sabbathday Lake, Maine. Those at Harvard, Sabbathday Lake, and Alfred are attributed on the basis of the Shakers' oral tradition; all the others are documented by manuscript and printed records. These ten meetinghouses were constructed in a mere nine years, between 1785 and 1794.

Considering the richness of this legacy and the reputation that Johnson enjoyed among his contemporaries, relatively

little is known of his life. The few facts that follow were gleaned chiefly from Shaker archives now at Canterbury. (Previous writers have been confused by the fact that there were three Shakers named Moses Johnson, but the archives make clear that the biographical material given here pertains to the builder.)

From the dates on his gravestone it can be established that Johnson was born in 1752, but the place of his birth is not recorded. He was living in the vicinity of Enfield, New Hampshire, when the Shakers started making converts there in 1782. In October of that year, when he was thirty years old, he entered the Society with his wife and three children. He was one of the original signers of the Enfield Covenant.

Johnson must have served his full apprenticeship as a carpenter and joiner and have had experience in these trades before he joined the Shakers. That he was no novice is indicated by the fact that in 1785, at the age of thirty-three, he was chosen by the Elders over all other Shakers to go to Mount Lebanon, a distance of over two hundred miles, where he was "given charge of framing the Church." Mount Lebanon had been the first fully organized community and was the center of the Shaker faith. Johnson supervised construction of its meetinghouse, and with the help of Shaker brethren from the Mount Lebanon families the frame was raised and assembled by October 15. It was then pine-clapboarded, roofed, and sufficiently completed inside so that the first service could be held in it on January 29, 1786.

Mount Lebanon was situated on a ridge along the New York-Massachusetts border, in New Lebanon township. On the flat, fertile Massachusetts farm land to the east lay the Hancock Shaker community. Moses Johnson moved his tools to Hancock after completing his work at Mount Lebanon and supervised the raising of the meetinghouse there. On August 30, 1786, the foundation was laid and in the following year the church was ready for use.

Johnson returned to Mount Lebanon for a time. In 1789 he built the first gristmill there and, as if to show his versatility, erected "a commodious Hogsty" the following year. He was then sent by the Elders to Watervliet, the site of the first Shaker settlement in 1776, and in 1791 he oversaw the erection of the church there. He began work in March of

Moses Johnson's first meetinghouse at Mount Lebanon, built 1785-1786, from a Lossing & Barritt wood engraving which appeared in *Harper's Monthly* for July 1857. It illustrates the style developed by Johnson at the very outset and used in all his other meetinghouses. Besides the two separate entrances for the brethren and sisters, this view shows the door at the left end by which the male ministry ascended their staircase to the living quarters on the second floor. The female members of the ministry had a similar entrance and staircase at the other end. *Photograph from Historic American Buildings Survey, Library of Congress.*

Of the surviving Moses Johnson Shaker meetinghouses, that at Sabbathday Lake (built in 1794) is in most nearly original condition. Of note are the English-style gambrel roof, double entrance doors for the brethren and sisters, the large single shutters, and the dormers. All the wood for the building was cut by the Shakers from their wood lots; they hand forged all the nails and made the bricks from clay on their property. *Photograph by John McKee, reproduced by courtesy of the president and trustees of Bowdoin College, copyright 1969.*

The typical Moses Johnson gambrel roof
is exemplified in the Sabbathday Lake meetinghouse.
The pitches are of about equal length,
and the lower one is steep.
The eaves return at both levels.
Photograph by Miller/Swift.

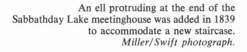

An ell protruding at the end of the
Sabbathday Lake meetinghouse was added in 1839
to accommodate a new staircase.
Miller/Swift photograph.

The first-floor meeting room of the Sabbathday Lake meetinghouse. Braced and boxed ceiling beams run the width of the ceiling. There are two peg boards let into the white plaster walls, and wainscoting extends up to the window sills. All the woodwork was painted a dark blue-green and the pine floors were yellow-white or yellow-ochre in color. The benches could be removed to permit the singing and dancing exercises which were part of the Shakers' religious services, and built-in benches were provided for spectators. *McKee photograph, by courtesy of Bowdoin College.*

This is the only known photograph of the interior of the original Hancock meetinghouse; it was taken about 1926. The building, built in 1786-1787, was razed in 1938. It was similar to the other Johnson churches except for the attractive paneled window embrasures. In the mid-nineteenth century it was remodeled and a pitch roof added; braces for the ceiling beams were removed and the beams themselves were covered by a false ceiling. *HABS photograph.*

that year, with the assistance of Brothers Moses Mixer, Stephen Markham, and John Bruce. Probably he stayed only long enough to supervise the laying of the foundation and the basic framing of the structure, since by June he was already in Enfield, Connecticut, working on the church there. The foundation of the Enfield meetinghouse may have been already completed to his specifications when he arrived because it is recorded that Moses, his helper, Nathan Farrington, and the Enfield brethren "calculated to raise" the frame on June 21. The church was completed by local Shakers the following year.

After the work at Enfield, Johnson traveled back to Watervliet to erect a blacksmith shop. Then he went on to Harvard to oversee the construction of a meetinghouse at this community, which had just been "gathered into gospel order." Moving north to New Hampshire, Johnson next

oversaw the erection of the frame for the Canterbury church. According to Elder Henry Blinn's journal, work started on May 9, 1792. Johnson stayed at Canterbury through the early summer and then returned to Massachusetts to undertake the planned meetinghouse at Shirley. Local Shaker brethren completed the Canterbury church on September 22, 1792.

Work at Shirley began in August and the frame was raised on October 31. Construction was resumed in the spring of 1793 and the building was ready for services in the fall. Father Eleazer Rand conducted the first meeting in the edifice on October 27.

From Shirley, Johnson returned to Enfield, New Hampshire, in 1793. There the Shakers had grown sufficiently in number to require a meetinghouse, and Johnson was again called on to supervise its erection.

The Shakers at Alfred had planned a new meetinghouse in 1791 and timber for it was cut and sawed the following year. The church was raised under Moses Johnson's direction and sufficiently completed so that it could be formally dedicated in 1793. The interior work was finished in 1794. At the end of 1794 Johnson went a few miles north to the other Maine Shaker settlement at Sabbathday Lake and oversaw the construction of that community's meetinghouse.

The tenth meetinghouse completed, Moses Johnson returned to Enfield, New Hampshire. Little is known of his later life. He served briefly as an Elder and died at the age of ninety on December 19, 1842. A lifelong Shaker, he is buried in the South Family Cemetery at Enfield.

The first Shaker meetinghouse that Johnson built, at Mount Lebanon, set the pattern for all those to follow. The Millennial Laws of the Shakers stated that their meetinghouses were the only buildings which could be painted white. This symbolically pure color set them apart from all other structures. To assure that they were even more distinctive, Moses Johnson designed them with a gambrel or hip roof, which gave a different silhouette from the gable or pitch roofs of the other Shaker buildings.

The gambrel roof is indeed the most distinctive feature of Johnson's meetinghouses. Superficially, they resemble colo-

By the time this photograph was taken, about 1920, the original Johnson meetinghouse at Watervliet was being used for storage, having been supplanted for religious services by the larger church, seen next to it, built in 1846. The building was demolished in 1927. This photograph illustrates the original sash arrangement found on nearly all the original meetinghouses: 12 over 12 lights on the first floor, 12 over 8 lights on the second, 6 over 6 lights on the third, and 6 over 6 lights on the dormers. *HABS photograph.*

Johnson's meetinghouse at Enfield, Connecticut (built 1791-1792), was different from the others in several respects. It appears larger and the massive chimneys suggest that the building was heated by fireplaces rather than the small Shaker stoves. The stair wells leading to the upstairs floors were entered from a doorway at the rear rather than at the front of the ends. The two small windows in the third-floor eaves, probably for closets, and the two other small windows in the attic storage area, were also unique features. The bell cupola is a later addition, a dormer has apparently been removed from the gambrel, and the asymmetrical fenestration of the façade indicates alterations. This photograph, probably the only one of the Enfield meetinghouse, was published in *The Connecticut Quarterly* for October and December 1897 (p. 461).

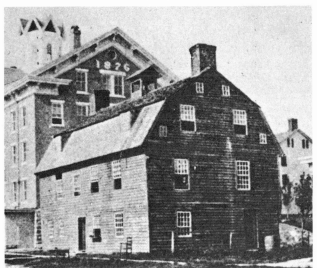

nial gambrel-roofed buildings in the Hudson River Valley, and it has been suggested that the Shaker churches show Dutch influence. However, the gambrel roof and braced ceiling beams, with both beams and braces boxed in, are as common in English architecture as in Dutch, and are found throughout southern New England, especially in Connecticut. Furthermore, the Dutch gambrel has a considerable overhang at the eaves, a very long first pitch, and a much shorter top pitch. Johnson employed pitches of about equal lengths, characteristics of the English hip roof. The steepness of the pitch that he used is also closer to the English-derived Connecticut gambrel than to the New York Dutch gambrel.

Moses Johnson's churches were all rectangular, nearly all five by two bays. On the long front façade were two doors, the left for brethren, the right for sisters. Three windows were placed between the doors, and two more at each end. The lower pitch of the gambrel roof was pierced by six

Although the Harvard meetinghouse (built 1791) had its original gambrel changed to a pitch roof and the interior was partitioned for residential use, the building still retains its original window arrangement, wide single shutters, and solid granite steps leading to the two entrances. Nearly all the Johnson churches employed large slab stone foundations, usually granite or ashlar, as seen here. The iron scroll-end handrails are characteristic of Harvard. *HABS photograph.*

Interior of the original Shirley meetinghouse, as now reconstructed at Hancock Shaker Village. In accordance with the Shakers' Millennial Laws, the woodwork of this room was painted a deep blue, the walls white. The pendent brass lighting fixtures were described by the Reverend William Bentley in 1795: "These brasses were flat plates not formed like our Chandeliers but to set candle sticks upon . . . They shove up, so as easily to be put entirely out of the way." *Photograph by Eugene Merrick Dodd.*

The meetinghouse at Shirley, built by Johnson in 1792-1793, remained in continuous use for religious services until the community was dissolved in 1908 due to a decline in membership. In 1962 the old church, still solid after more than a century and a half, was partially disassembled and moved across the state to Hancock, where it was rebuilt on the site of the original meetinghouse there. This photograph shows it as restored. *Dodd photograph.*

dormers, three on each side. There were two chimneys at the ridge, one at each end.

The interiors were designed to fit specific needs. The first floor had to be given over, in its entirety, to a large meeting room where the Shakers could conduct their services. Upstairs rooms had to be provided for the members of the ministry who were privileged to live in the meetinghouse. Besides having two entrances, the meetinghouses had two staircases for the male and female ministers, and two separate sets of two-room living quarters on the second floor. At some of the communities, the half-floor under the ridge was finished off to provide two additional guest rooms for visiting Shaker Elders and Eldresses from other communities.

The Millennial Laws specifically stated that the interior woodwork should be "of a blueish shade." This was interpreted by the Shakers as a dark blue-green or Prussian blue which made a striking contrast with the white plastered walls and the yellow-white or yellow-ochre floors.

In the first-floor meeting room there was invariably wooden wainscoting, in the style of colonial buildings, which extended to the height of the window sills and was topped with a chair rail. Above the wainscoting, at a height of about five or six feet, were two or more rows of wooden pegs set into narrow boards.

The ceiling of the meeting room was distinguished by the boxed ceiling beams, across the width of the structure, supported by boxed knee braces. Around the front periphery of the room were two or three raised levels of benches, painted chocolate brown. These were reserved for spectators from the "world" who wished to watch the Shakers' Sabbath services. The brethren and sisters themselves sat on movable benches ranged in the center of the floor, which were easily removed for the dancing exercises. The pipes of two small Shaker stoves entered the two chimneys at the ends of the room, except at Enfield, Connecticut, where the meetinghouse was probably heated by fireplaces, if one may judge from the unusually large chimneys it had.

The two staircases were originally placed at either end of the building, but as more and more "world" people became interested in the Shakers it was found necessary in some of the meetinghouses to remove the stair wells in order to provide additional space for the spectators' benches. This resulted, at both Sabbathday Lake and Canterbury, in building on an ell to accommodate a new staircase. The one at Canterbury, added in 1815, was placed at the rear and so does not detract from the symmetry and balance of the façade. The one at Sabbathday Lake, built in 1839, protrudes from one end and looks like the afterthought it is. However, it affords a gentler ascent to the second floor than the very steep staircase at Canterbury.

The meetinghouse at Sabbathday Lake is today as perfect as the day it was built. The original dark blue woodwork has never been repainted since it was applied by Johnson in

1794. Because of this, and because it has never been altered for use as anything other than a church, it best illustrates how all the Moses Johnson meetinghouses appeared when first constructed.

In the church at Canterbury, now used as a museum, the meeting room was repainted a light blue by Elder Henry Blinn about 1875. The upstairs rooms are still in their original dark blue and retain an unusual feature—interior "Indian" shutters which recess by sliding into the walls.

The only other Johnson church still intact is the one from Shirley. Moved from that community in 1962, it now stands, carefully restored, at Hancock Shaker Village on the site of that community's original meetinghouse. It is the only Johnson meetinghouse extant with the original interior staircases.

Sad fates have overtaken the other meetinghouses. The one at Alfred was destroyed by fire in 1902. That at Enfield, New Hampshire, was sold about 1900 to Louis St. Gaudens, brother of the sculptor Augustus St. Gaudens, and moved to a hilltop near Cornish, New Hampshire, where it still stands, but greatly altered. The Harvard church received a gable roof in the mid-nineteenth century and the interior was partitioned for residential purposes; it is privately owned today. The one at Enfield, Connecticut, became a hospital for the Shakers and was demolished between 1876 and 1880. The Watervliet meetinghouse came to be too small, and after a larger church was erected in 1846 it was employed for storage and finally demolished about 1927, when the Shakers sold some of their property to Albany County for use as a county home. The original Hancock meetinghouse had its roof raised in the nineteenth century and was razed in 1938. At Mount Lebanon, after a new and larger church was erected in 1824, the old meetinghouse was remodeled: an additional story was added, a gable roof was installed, and the building became successively a seed house and a storage shed. Again extensively remodeled, it now serves as the residence for the headmaster of the Darrow School, which owns most of the Mount Lebanon properties.

Probably no single man contributed as much as Moses Johnson to the character we have come to associate with Shaker architecture. Since the meetinghouses were the center of Shaker life, their simple, dignified appearance established the standard for other buildings that were constructed as the communities grew.

For invaluable assistance with this article, I want to thank Eldress Marguerite Frost of Canterbury and Sister R. Mildred Barker of Sabbathday Lake.

This view of the Shirley meetinghouse, taken when it was partially disassembled in 1962, shows the massive timbers used by Johnson as the main members of the frame. Visible here is the series of great braces mortised and pegged into the ceiling beams and vertical frame members. They were later covered by sheathing, as may be seen in the interior view of the Sabbathday Lake meetinghouse. *HABS photograph.*

This detail from an 1853 wood engraving shows the Canterbury Church Family buildings with Moses Johnson's gambrel-roofed meetinghouse at the right. Because of its matchless hilltop location Canterbury is renowned as one of the most beautifully situated Shaker communities. *From* Illustrated News, *October 29, 1853; collection of the author.*

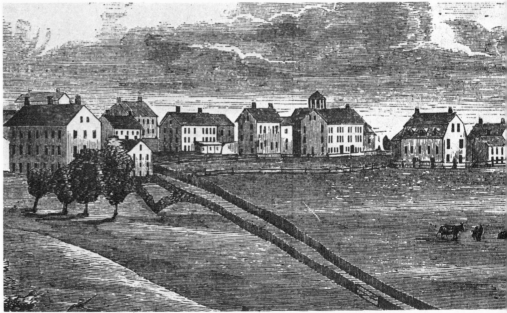

Micajah Burnett and the buildings at Pleasant Hill

BY JAMES C. THOMAS, *Curator, Shakertown, Kentucky*

A SHAKER SCRIBE who knew Micajah Burnett said of him, "He was the principal architect of this village; an accomplished civil engineer, a masterly mathematician . . . a mechanic and machinist of the first order . . . and withal a firmly established honest hearted Christian Shaker beloved, respected and honored by all."

Born in Patrick County, Virginia, in 1791, Micajah was the first of four children of Benjamin and Elizabeth Burnett. A second child, Charity, was born in 1792 while the family was still living in Virginia. Thereafter the Burnetts joined the westward movement and migrated to Wayne County, Kentucky, where two more sons were born to them, Andrew in 1799 and Zachiah in 1801. The records at Pleasant Hill show that Benjamin and Elizabeth Burnett accepted the Shaker beliefs in 1808, and that the four children "believed" in 1809.

The Pleasant Hill Shaker community in Kentucky began in 1805 when three Mercer County farmers were converted to the faith and settled on a farm belonging to one of them, Elisha Thomas, about a mile from the present village. The earliest buildings were crude structures and none exist today.

The first permanent building in the village was constructed in 1809 as the dwelling house for the Center Family. This two-and-a-half-story structure was built of stone in a broken ashlar pattern and has two end chimneys with fireplace openings on the first and second floors. It contains one large room downstairs, and on the floor above several small rooms made by installing thin board partitions. The building was used as a tavern after 1817 and it is believed that the partitions were installed at that time. Later it was used as the Farm Deacon's Shop and it is so called today.

Elder Henry C. Blinn of the Canterbury community mentioned Burnett in an account of his visit to Pleasant Hill in 1873: "Br. Micajah invites us to visit his shop.— He now lives at the age of 81 yrs in a building that he framed when he was 17 yrs old."

Little biographical information about Micajah Burnett is available but we are certain that he had no formal architectural training. He must have had an innate sense of design, and some practical training as a carpenter and joiner, and apparently he used handbooks on architecture to supplement his creative skills. Elder Blinn remarked, "In his shop we found a large library of excellent books." He became the master carpenter, architect, and town planner of Pleasant Hill, and lent his services on occasion to other communities as well.

In 1813 Burnett replaced the original village plan of putting the important buildings on a north-south axis with one which situated them on an east-west road. The East Family House, built in 1817, was the first of the large

dwelling houses to be constructed on the present village road. It is a massive brick structure built in a T shape, three and one-half stories high in the front with two floors in the back. A similar T plan was used in the Center Family House and the West Family House, the two other dwellings of the senior or church order.

Double entrance doors and separate staircases (even to the cellars) were used in all the dwelling houses to facilitate the separation of the sexes. The sisters resided on the right side of the house and the brethren on the left. Their "retiring rooms," located in the front and middle of the buildings, were large enough to accommodate three or four beds, a chest of drawers, and several chairs, and were used only for sleeping.

Sick members were confined to the infirmary, a separate

Micajah Burnett, architect of Pleasant Hill. An early sketch by C. S. Rafinesque, professor of natural history at Transylvania University in Lexington, Kentucky. *Transylvania University Library.*

The Farm Deacon's Shop, built in 1809, is the oldest building in the village. It was first a dwelling house, later a tavern and is now used as a craft shop. Interesting features are its irregular ashlar stonework and original ash floors. *Photograph by Linda Hockensmith.*

The East Family House is the oldest family residence at Pleasant Hill. Built in 1817, this large, roomy structure is of brick laid in Flemish bond, with stone foundations, crown-mold gutter, raised-panel doors and jambs, and separate doors and stairways for men and women. *Except as noted, illustrations are by courtesy of the Kentucky Department of Public Information; photographs by Kalman Papp.*

area at the rear of the building on the second floor. The dining room was located on the first floor between the sleeping quarters and the kitchen. The meeting room was directly above the dining room.

The West Family House, intended for the older members of the community, followed the East Family dwelling four years later (1821) and is very similar in design, though smaller. The brick is laid in Flemish bond and rests on a bushhammered stone foundation. Like the East Family

House, it has bold raised panels on the exterior doors and jambs, and stone steps. Here, Micajah first used the attractive interior arched doorway which was later repeated in the Center Family House.

The meetinghouse was constructed in 1820, approximately in the center of the village. A newspaper correspondent from Virginia visiting Pleasant Hill in 1825 described the building this way: "The church is a frame building underpinned with superior neatness with stone;

One of the twin spiral stairways
in the Trustees' House at Pleasant Hill, Kentucky,
built by Micajah Burnett in 1839–1840.
Shakertown; photograph by H. J. Scheirich III.

The Meetinghouse was constructed in 1820. It is 60 by 44 feet and rests upon a heavy limestone foundation. The walls are an intricate framework of heavy studding and plates of hewn timbers. Roof and ceilings are supported or suspended on a series of interlocking cantilever-type trusses and overhead studdings and rafters. The Shakers held their worship services in the large room on the first floor and the ministry used the second floor as living quarters.

The limestone Center Family House, erected between 1824 and 1834, is the largest structure. The front section measures 55 by 60 feet, the dining room and kitchen wing 34 by 85 feet. It has square gabled ends and three massive chimneys. Now the Shaker Museum, it was once the residence of one hundred Shakers.

Central hall in Center Family House.
Double doors with raised panels, which lead to the cellar,
were for the separate sexes.
Arched doorways may be seen in right and left foreground.
Floors are white oak.

it is about sixty feet long and proportionately wide, plastered and white washed, with chairboards, &c painted blue, in the neatest conceivable style."

In accordance with Shaker practice, the outside of the meetinghouse was white, and it was the only frame building in the village painted in this manner. All other clapboard buildings were red or yellow; the latter color predominated. The lower floor contains the meeting room where the devotional dances were performed. Movable benches were provided for the worshipers, while benches secured to the walls—called fasteners—accommodated spectators. The second floor was divided into apartments for the Elders and Eldresses. Splendid white-oak framing in the attic "suspends" the ceiling of the first floor, eliminating the need for interior supports that would interfere with the spirited dancing.

The largest building in the village, the Center Family House, was home to approximately a hundred members and took ten years to complete. According to an original temporal journal: "on . . . May 21, 1824 the foundation of the large stone building opposite the Meeting House . . . was laid . . . The walls were erected in 1825. It was covered and some other work done on it in 1826 and 1827. And in 1834 it was finished off and the family moved into it on the 24 of September of that year."

White limestone, known locally as Kentucky marble, was quarried less than a mile from the village on the bluffs of the Kentucky River. The stone is laid in regular courses, each block showing a beautifully tooled face. The molded window sills were made of sandstone and painted white. The floors in this building, as in most dwelling houses, were made of ash and oak with a natural finish. The ceilings were high, which helped keep the building cool in summer.

The balanced fenestration and central-hall plan may be described as Shaker Georgian (by this time domestic architecture in Kentucky was deep in the Greek revival period). Engaged columns and a paneled wainscot in the dining room represent the first use of "worldly" decoration. The meeting room, which has a curved ceiling, plastered cornice, and paneled wainscot, might also be considered elaborate within the context of Shaker strictures.

The year 1833 marked the completion of the water system at Pleasant Hill under the direction of Micajah Burnett. This was the first public waterworks west of the Allegheny Mountains, and provided every house and barn in the village with running water. The Water House, a yellow frame building, contains a large cypress tank mounted on stone piers. Interior walls have brick nogging laid between the framing members for insulation. When the system was functioning a float located in the center of the tank protruded through the roof and was visible from the pump house in the tanyard a half mile below the village. The floating gauge would go down with the water level, indicating to the operator when to start the horse-driven pump.

Micajah's success with the Pleasant Hill water system did not go unnoticed by the other Kentucky Shaker settlement, South Union, near Auburn. A South Union scribe stated: ". . . Micajah Burnett arrived here from Pleasant Hill, whose business is to the oversight, direction and management of the business relating to our contemplated Water Works."

A corner of the meeting room on the second floor of the Center Family House. Note plaster cornice molding and curved ceiling. White window prop can be seen in jamb of window opening. *Hockensmith photograph.*

Meeting-room door in the Center Family House has arched fanlight with gothic muntins. The area beyond the door was the infirmary. Paneled wainscot can be seen at lower right. *Hockensmith photograph.*

Construction of the Trustees' House was begun in 1839 and finished in late 1840. Intended to house the "world's people" who came to transact business with the Shakers, it is without a doubt the most elegant structure at Pleasant Hill, perhaps in all Shakerdom. Twin spiral staircases rise seemingly unsupported to the third floor (see frontispiece). Three-inch white-oak stair risers are firmly secured with large bolts. The wood trim, including baseboards, was painted light brown, offering an interesting contrast to the dwelling houses, where most of the trim was painted various shades of "Shaker blue" and the baseboards a brick red. The plaster walls were white.

Pinboards, or peg rails, were used in this building, as in all the others, for hanging chairs, mirrors, sconces, clothing, and the like. The thousands of pins, turned by hand, were as aesthetically pleasing as they were utilitarian. The massive Pleasant Hill buildings have high ceilings and the pinboards serve to break the monotonous expanse between chair rail and ceiling.

The 1840's were busy building years for the Shakers at Pleasant Hill, but the structures of this period are for the most part small and of undistinguished design. The West Family Wash House was put up in 1842, followed by the West Family Sisters' Shop in 1844. The East Family Brethren's Shop was begun in 1845 and the Post Office in 1848. Micajah Burnett was still the general planner and overseer for the village, but his activity was greatly reduced. The important work had been done. Other men with lesser ability were put in charge and Micajah became the principal trading deacon for Pleasant Hill.

The Shakers were famous for their garden seed, flat brooms, and pure medicinal herbs. These products, along with furniture, raw silk, and preserves, were sold from wagons or shipped down-river to New Orleans, the principal market of the Kentucky communities before the Civil War. Trusted trading deacons traveled for many months of the year making the name Shaker known as a standard of excellence. One village scribe wrote in December 24, 1859: "This morning Micajah Burnett returned home from New Orleans and wherever else he has been; it appears from the face of the journal that Micajah has been from home the past 6 months and 12 days."

During Burnett's years of traveling he recruited many children to replenish the dwindling number in the community. Some stayed and became valuable adult members; but most left, finding the Shaker life too hard. For example, "Joseph Middleton left this society for this wicked world, he will be 22 years of age day after tomorrow, we have raised him from a small boy. . . Micajah Burnett got him at New Orleans."

Burnett's name does not appear very often in the temporal journals of the 1860's, and one may surmise that his duties had been lightened due to his advancing age. He was sixty-nine in 1860 and had served his fellow members at Pleasant Hill for more than fifty years. A scant reference in the Church Record under the heading "Change" affirms the fact that he continued to work until 1872: "Brother Micajah retires from all connection with business at the Post Office."

Elder Henry Blinn's account of his visit to Pleasant Hill the following year contains several interesting passages about Micajah: "At 9 o'clock we accompanied our aged Brother Micajah on the road to the Kentucky River." On the way they stopped by the East Family House to see the silkworms. Referring to the road to the river Blinn stated: "Brother Micajah projected this great work and had the whole management till the job was finished." Further on he wrote: "The walk was very pleasant and the scenery beautiful. We walked slowly along but the excessive heat with the Journey was more than our aged father could endure. For a few minutes he became bewildered and we were obliged to have him rest under the shade of a large tree." Four or five days later Blinn was taken to the belfrey of the Center Family House to look at the magnificent view of the countryside. "Brother Micajah," said Blinn, "accompanied us on this trip and thought we should remove our shoes before we went out on the roof."

Burnett was now in absolute retirement and remained in good health until his death in 1879. A terse entry appeared in a journal dated Tuesday, December 7, 1878: "Micajah Burnett dangerously ill." This was followed by record of his death on Friday, January 10, 1879: "Micajah Burnett breathed his last 20 minutes past 9:00 a.m." He was buried in the village graveyard at two o'clock the following day. The twenty-three surviving buildings in the restored Shaker village of Pleasant Hill, Kentucky, stand today as a monument to him.

The Water House, built in 1833, was a portion of the first public waterworks west of the Alleghenies. The Shakers pumped water by horse power from a spring by the Tanyard House, a distance of 1800 feet with an elevation of 125 feet. The building is frame and the walls have brick nogging, covered by mitered weatherboards painted yellow. Inside is a cypress tank with a capacity of 4400 gallons, mounted on stone piers.

The Trustees' House, begun in 1839, is one of the most beautiful buildings at Pleasant Hill. It was used by the Shakers for transacting business with the "world" and for meals and lodging for guests. It contains five dining rooms and twelve guest rooms and is now used as an inn. The building is of Flemish-bond brick with incised-line mortar joints, and there is evidence of white painted lines between the bricks. It has louvered blinds painted green, dormers, and fine cornice moldings.

III Furniture

This comparatively long section, devoted to the furniture of the Shakers, is appropriate in several ways. We can see simplicity of line, grace, harmony, and balance in these handcrafted objects and realize that these attributes were all implicit in the Shakers' faith. That Edward Deming Andrews and his wife, Faith, wrote between them five out of eight of these articles is also as it should be. Our interest in the Shakers during the past fifty years has been largely stimulated by their research and writing. They awakened our appreciation and added to our awareness of this extraordinary movement. When the Andrewses first visited Hancock in 1923, they reported: "We found the Shakers the friendliest of people, sincere, hospitable, and, once their confidence was won, helpful beyond measure. Led to believe that the routine of years had stereotyped them, we found them a very human people; nor had individuality been obliterated by the communal system. There was humor here, and breadth of interest, and above all, a quality best described as simple goodness." We are fortunate that the Andrewses' hearts were in their work, just as was so true of the Shakers themselves, the product of whose hearts and hands reflected "that faithful improvement of talents" which they sought.

When these 'faculties are exercised in divine worship, God is honored and glorified by them. (*The Millennial Church,* Part II, Chapter V.)

The Shakers in a new world

BY EDWARD D. ANDREWS

COLLECTING ANTIQUES IS A HIGHLY PERSONAL adventure, and in forming our collection of materials related to the Shakers my wife and I have learned its pleasures, problems, and rewards. Yet it is with utmost satisfaction that we now transfer the enterprise we undertook as individuals to an institution which will expand its usefulness.

We began back in the 1920's when, with a general interest in the antiques of our region, we came by chance on the Shaker community at Hancock, Massachusetts, and bought one chair, then a few other pieces of furniture. At first we were not aware that we had happened

Shaker tin and pewter cupboard of pine, painted dark red; from the New Lebanon Church family. The chest is a tailoring counter with drop leaf, from the Watervliet community. Top and drawer fronts are curly maple; side panels, pine; original red stain. The (non-Shaker) portrait was found in Richmond, Massachusetts.

on a distinct type or school of American craftsmanship. There was no literature on the subject. What collecting had been done was confined to the characteristic web-seated chairs, product of an early Shaker industry, and a few trestle dining tables which, coming into the market under the guise of primitive American pieces, had lost their identity. Before long, however, we discovered that the Believers made all their own furnishings, not only chairs and tables but chests, cupboards, tailoring counters, benches and stools, stands, beds, desks, clocks, mirrors, small cabinetwork, stoves, utensils—in fact, all the equipment of their communal homes, churches, schoolhouses, offices, and shops.

Our initial aim was the acquisition of all types of household furniture and accessories made by the Shakers, in the pursuit of which we gradually extended activity to the New York State communities at New Lebanon and Watervliet, and then to the societies in Connecticut, Maine, and New Hampshire. Interest broadened in time to include the furnishings and products of the varied Shaker shops, most of them long disused but filled with the paraphernalia of industry. Meanwhile we began to collect communitarian literature. The followers of Mother Ann Lee were assiduous publicists and keepers of journals and records, and their buildings held a wealth of printed and written documents. The search was irresistible, the lure ever-expanding.

As time passed and the material accumulated, we became more and more concerned about its eventual disposition. The alternatives of whether, and how, to preserve, or whether to disperse and thereby create opportunity for future collecting, have been faced by others, but for us there was a complicating factor. Our collection told the complex story of a productive culture that constituted a rich strain in American historical experience, and in scope, authenticity, and documentation could probably never be duplicated. To consider it as an exclusively personal possession became increasingly difficult. More or less consciously, we came to the view that had been held by the Shakers themselves, that property was a trust, a heritage to be used and "improved" under responsible stewardship.

What Yale University and a few other colleges were beginning to do in using works of art as teaching collections, and in integrating the history of art with actual laboratory and museum experience, suggested a solution to our problem. And concurrently, what we had been trying to do, in articles, books, and exhibitions, to interpret the Shaker material had come to the attention of the School of Fine Arts and the American Studies Program at Yale. This program, begun in 1950, is a pioneer project which comprises "a general course of study

*Illustrations from the Andrews collection,
by courtesy of the Yale Art Gallery;
photographs by Robert J. Kelley.*

Six-dawer pine counter, with top and base moldings, from the New Lebanon Church family. Shaker oval boxes, wall sconce, and cobbler's candlestand. The landscape is a "plan" of the Poland (Maine) community drawn by Joshua H. Bussell of Alfred, January 1, 1850.

Trustees' desk, pine stained with a thin pink wash, from the Second Order of the New Lebanon Church. The lids rest on a sill. One-slat chairs were originally used in the Shaker dining rooms. Beside the desk is a high-seated shop chair.

The care expended on even the humblest pieces is illustrated by this pine washstand, from the North family at New Lebanon. The wooden disk for holding the slop pail is mortised into a post which swivels for convenient use. The rocking chair (finished in mahogany) is a relatively late but dignified product of the chair shops at the Second and South families, New Lebanon. From the rod at the top could be hung a cushion or mat. The wooden screen was originally used in the "nurse shop" or infirmary of the New Lebanon Church. The framed photograph is of the late Sister Sadie Neale, Church family deaconess.

Dr. Andrews is consultant on Shaker history and culture at Yale.

in every aspect of American History, political, economic, social, artistic, philosophical, and religious." One of its principal objectives is, in the words of Professor David M. Potter, "to foster an awareness of the richness and range of the American experience." It is an experiment in general education, or what used to be called the liberal arts.

One of the claims of the American Studies project was "that a particular civilization or culture, with all its diversity, has a certain underlying homogeneity, perhaps a spirit, which can serve as a unifying key to the interpretation of its diverse phenomena." Creative use of the Shaker material can demonstrate the validity of such a claim: for with all its diversity, one is conscious of the underlying spirit that gives it unity. At the same time, a broad understanding of the whole is dependent on a study of its parts, not only the selected artifacts themselves but the literature which gives them meaning. The Shaker order was a microcosmic civilization, a laboratory of social experiment largely removed from the world. Thoroughly documenting this important chapter in American cultural history, our collection offers an integrated unit for study in accord with the philosophy and purpose of the Yale program.

For the student of design and its history, the section devoted to furniture has particular value as an early expression, perhaps the earliest in the country, of an indigenous style of craftsmanship—original forms which

Weave chest, with sill, of grained pine, from the New Lebanon "wash house" or laundry. The rim-top serving table, of mixed woods, has a large drawer in front and a narrow one at each end. The inspirational *Tree of Life* was "seen and painted" by Sister Hannah Cahoon of Hancock on July 3, 1854.

Splay-leg drop-leaf table from the New Lebanon Church, showing typical leg turning. Curly-maple "tilting" chair, with tape seat and metal ball-and-socket device at base of rear posts. The pipe rack, with tin tray, holds Shaker-made pipes.

Shaker rocking chairs customarily had four slats, with ladle arms or (as here) mushrooms at the top of the front posts. The wood is maple and cherry. Shape of finials and type of seat often provide a clue to date and provenance: this is a No. 3 tape-seated chair made at New Lebanon in the mid-nineteenth century. The "round stand" of cherry is a delicate piece from the Second family at New Lebanon. On it is a white-poplar sewing basket.

bore (in Horatio Greenough's words) "an organic relation with God's ground." Unnoticed by the world, the Shakers were applying, during the first half of the nineteenth century, certain principles regarding essential form and function which were later to be advocated by Ruskin, Morris, and Eastlake in England, and in America by the sculptor Greenough, the architect Louis Sullivan, and, in philosophical context, even by Emerson and Whitman. Considered thus, Shaker artifacts represent more than an assemblage of antiques as such, however integrated and pleasing to the eye: they demonstrate in clearest focus the doctrine that use (or function) and order (or organization) are true components of the beautiful.

That the doctrine of "good use" and order was essentially a moral or religious one gives Shaker craftsmanship added significance. In his *Way-Marks* (c. 1790) Joseph Meacham, the organizer of the Millennial Church, insisted that "all things must be made . . . according to their order and use," and that "All work done, or things made in the church, ought to be faithfully and well done, but plain and without superfluity—neither too high nor too low." It was a basic principle that "That which has in itself the highest use possesses the greatest beauty," and a favorite quotation that "Order is heaven's first law." Whether applied to noble or common uses, to meetinghouses or shops, to tables for the ministry or looms and reels for the weaver, the work of the hands

was an act of integrity, of faith. Though the Shakers of New England, New York, and the Ohio-Kentucky frontier inherited certain craft traditions from their forebears, as separatists faced with the challenge of a new and better start they rejected anything suggestive of worldly vanity and pretense, and as perfectionists sought to free their work from "all error or blemish." In the process they developed not only "vernacular" forms, as John A. Kouwenhoven has aptly called them, "without any reference to the cultivated tradition," but forms with a purity of line symbolic of their religious convictions.

At the Yale Art Gallery the furniture, pictures, and other artifacts will be displayed as distinct groupings to illustrate various types of Shaker craft and art. The gallery itself, a spacious, well-lighted, rectangular room, will recreate a Shaker meeting room, with white walls, blue peg boards, moldings, and doors, and, at one end, the benches, windows, and paneled window frames from the eighteenth-century church at Hancock. Changing exhibits will be supplemented by a catalogue documenting the date, provenance, and use of every item in the collection, and by a library of manuscripts, books, pamphlets, and pictorial material useful in the fields not only of graphic art, design, and architecture, but also of music, drama, sociology, economics, and religion. Here, in a congenial atmosphere, the student can learn of the work and gain insight into the spirit of an inspired American folk.

Five-drawer sewing cabinet with drop leaf, from Hancock; mixed woods, brown stain. The tinware and brush are Shaker-made. Wall clock by Isaac N. Youngs, New Lebanon, 1840.

Pine cupboard-case, with original yellow stain; New Lebanon Church family. Two-step stool, used to reach the high drawers and cupboards of many Shaker pieces. Small drop-leaf table, in cherry, on which rests a rack of drawers faced in curly maple. Typical small pine bench. On the wall is an etching of a Shaker stove, by Armin Landeck.

Fig. 1 — Shaker Chairs

Craftsmanship of an American Religious Sect

Notes on Shaker Furniture

By Edward A. and Faith Andrews

Illustrations mainly from the authors' collection

NOTE. For the benefit of those who may have no reference book immediately at hand, it may be well to state that the Shakers, properly known as the United Society of Believers in Christ's Second Appearing, were a sect founded by Anne Lee of Manchester, England, between 1760 and 1770. In 1774 the founder and a small group of followers emigrated to America, where they first settled near Albany, New York. Despite many early hardships, the sect prospered after the Revolution, and, by

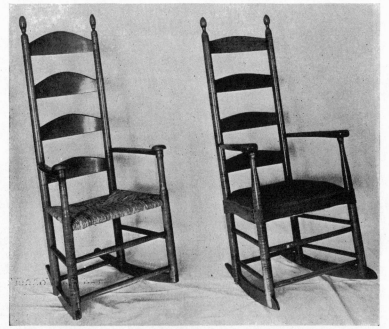

Fig. 2 — Shaker Rocking-Chairs
Turnings of carefully selected curly maple. The age of such pieces is not determinable. The similarity to earlier Colonial types is obvious.

1870, boasted some eighteen distinct communities, scattered through Connecticut, Kentucky, Maine, Massachusetts, New York, New Hampshire, and Ohio.

The products of Shaker industry were by no means restricted to utilization by members of the sect. Indeed, cloth from Shaker looms, garments wrought by Shaker fingers, and innumerable other articles of one kind and another, made in Shaker shops, were vigorously merchandised wherever there was prospect of a market.

Fig. 3 — SHAKER TRESTLE TABLE
Quite probably of the nineteenth century, but similar in many respects to very early American tables. The fiddle-shaped supports constitute one point of departure from early types. The high placement of the stretcher is another characteristic not common to early tables.

Mr. Andrews, author of the following notes, possesses a *Catalogue and Price List of Chairs* issued not long after the Centennial Exhibition of 1875 by the Shaker Community of Mount Lebanon, New York. The introduction to this catalogue emphasizes the fact that "the Shakers were pioneers in the (chairmaking) business and perhaps the very first to engage in the business after the establishment of the independence of the country." The public is further warned that various outside manufacturers have made and offered imitations of Shaker chairs.

The chairs pictured in the catalogue are, without exception, simple slat-backs, with or without rockers. One feature of them upon which the catalogue lays stress is a webbing, interlaced to give a checkerboard effect, which is used to cushion seats and backs.

The chair prices quoted run from $4.50 each to $17.50 each. The styles shown are hardly comparable in excellence with those depicted in the illustrations accompanying this article. Even the Shakers appear to have yielded something to the demands of an era of bad taste. *The Editor.*

The especial interest which attaches itself to the craftsmanship of the Shakers is due mainly to the fact that it was a direct expression of the life and thought of a whole group of people. Even though this craftsmanship was probably in the main adaptive in character, it represented a common feeling toward life markedly in contrast with the individualistic artistic exhibitions of the "world," from which these spiritually-minded but industrious people sought to escape.

Each community furnished its dwellings with appointments closely related in general design and purpose, whose variations never transgressed the laws of that innate simplicity which these people applied to their dress, their dwellings, and their mode of living. In the "world," fine furniture was made for those who appreciated it or could afford to buy it. The Shakers made furniture for themselves — it was a natural expression of a natural need.

It is not the purpose here to enquire closely into the origins of Shaker manufacture. Engrossed as these people were in the task of maintaining themselves in a world hostile or indifferent to their ideals, their early records speak chiefly of the great pulsating force in their lives — their religion. We read of their "hearts to prayer," but we cannot accurately trace the intricate origins of their program, "hands to work." No doubt they were required to construct household furniture on a fairly large scale soon after they came to this country in the latter part of the eighteenth century — 1774, to be exact. Converts to the sect often brought their personal effects into the order, but, sooner or later, the Shakers themselves had to supply their furnishings.

The infrequent references to the subject which one finds in Shaker literature indicate that among the earliest craftsmen, in some of the communities at least, cabinetmakers were included. When the Shirley, Massachusetts, settlement was bought by the State, Sister Josephine, in recalling the early history of that community, mentioned this occupation in her list of industries. J. R. MacLean, in his *Shakers of Ohio*,* refers to the following vocations in Union Village, in 1819: blacksmithing, masonry, stonecutting, carpentry, tanning,

*Columbus, Ohio, 1907, p. 66.

Fig. 4 — SHAKER KITCHEN TABLE
Of mixed woods, with maple drop-leaf top.

fulling, clothing, cabinetmaking, tailoring, weaving, carding, and spinning. Clara Endicott Sears found among the Shaker journals at Harvard, Massachusetts, an account of chairs made there in 1843.* By 1874 an illustrated catalogue of Shaker chairs, footbenches, floor mats, and so on, made at Mount Lebanon, New York, had been published, indicating that there the commercial possibilities of manufacturing furniture for outside consumers had been recognized.

Even though no distinct record exists, it is quite probable that, in the early days of the Society in America, every important permanent community to some extent constructed its own furniture. For instance — though a careful examination of the local history of Enfield, Connecticut, reveals no reference to such an industry — a great deal of furniture is known to have been made in the town. As time went on and the communities spread (and, later, as they decreased and concentrated), an interchange of supplies and workmen furnished aid in places where there had previously been little, if any, provision for making furniture. This helped also to standardize the original type-forms. Some light on the general question of when and where the furniture was made may be shed, therefore, by a reference to the order in which the communities were established.

The later history of the Shakers reveals more clearly

*Gleanings from Shaker Journals, Boston, Houghton Mifflin Co., 1916, p. 232.

Fig. 5 — SMALL TABLES OR LIGHT STANDS
Apparently in native walnut. The legs of Shaker tripod tables are usually cut in profile and do not show the molded form common to "worldly" types of the better sort.

the outstanding centres of manufacture, such as Mount Lebanon, New York, where chairs were probably first made, and later patented for commercial purposes, and where the industry, in spite of limited resources, still survives.

In the absence of available sources of information, the interesting problem of how just such and such styles were created must be answered indirectly. A study of the characteristic forms of Shaker furniture suggests the hypothesis that the early craftsmen adapted to their own designs existing Colonial models before them. The Shaker chairs (Figs. 1 and 2)* may well have been directly derived from Colonial slatbacks; the trestle-board tables (Fig. 3) and light stands (Fig. 5), from their early American prototypes. In like manner, the dropleaf tables (Fig. 4), chests of drawers (Fig. 12), beds (Fig. 11), and stools (Fig. 10) suggest an undeniable affinity to earlier forms.

Other evidences of adaptation may be adduced from the occasional light stands with drawers (Fig. 9), the turnings of bedposts, the Windsor-type cross stretcher in stools (Fig. 10), the "bread-board" feature of certain table tops (Fig. 7), and the mushroom turning on the front posts of certain chair types (Fig. 2). Plainly borrowed, also,

Fig. 6 — SHAKER BLANKET CHEST (1837)
A solidly built, well dovetailed piece. On the back is inscribed *Made April 1837, Canaan* (New York).

*The back legs of Shaker side chairs were often fitted at the base with an ingenious half ball of wood (sometimes of brass) joined in a socket by a thong, an arrangement which permitted the sitter to tip back easily or even to rock. Rockers were used early in the Shaker chair industry, an indication that austerity of belief did not imply undue asceticism in their manners and modes of living.

Fig. 7 (left) — SHAKER
TABLE
The top has been reduced
in size. Original dimen-
sions, 34″ by 23″. Height
of table, 24″.

Fig. 8 (right) — SHAKER
MIRROR FRAME AND
RACK
The former is of maple;
the latter of maple and
cherry. The mirror rested
on the groove at the front
of the rack, and was held
in place by a cord passing
through a ring in the
mirror frame and attached
to a similar ring at the top
of the rack. The function
of the peg was to give the
mirror an outward tilt.

is the general idea of the rare bureau-desks, as well as the broad features of Shaker slant-top desks, blanket chests (*Fig. 6*), stretcher-base kitchen tables, candle-stands, and ironware.

It may be charged that the Shakers therefore origi-nated no new designs and were not a creative people. In a sense this is true; but they were by no means mere copyists. In discarding all unnecessary embellishment and artifice, they reduced these earlier designs to their essentials of form and proportion, and, in so doing, achieved distinctly beautiful results. Let it be noted, too, that the Shaker craftsmen chose their most beautiful woods, used skillfully their richest homemade dyes, and were fond of the effect which the color of garden flowers

made against the plain backgrounds of walls and dwell-ings and in contrast with the natural patina of wood surfaces.*

Ready at hand were trees of plain and curly maple, birch, chestnut, butternut, and honey pine. These were sawed and planed and turned into elements which, finally, were as masterfully and conscientiously assembled, pegged and doweled together as ever joiner labored. The craftsmen were satisfied with none but the best tools and the best resultant quality. They constituted, in a

*The vogue for finishing furniture "in the natural" was anticipated by the Shakers a century ago. Originally the natural wood was said to have been treated with aqua vitæ; later, shellac, mixed with a little chrome yellow, was used; then developed the practice of dipping chairs, stools, and so forth, in vats of dye made from butternut bark.

Fig. 9 (left) — SHAKER STAND
WITH DRAWER
The raised molded edge of
the top suggests certain
tables of French derivation.

Fig. 10 (right) — SHAKER
REVOLVING STOOL
Turnings evidently bor-
rowed from those of
Windsor chairs. The seat
revolves, but is not adjustable, as the iron supporting rod has no thread.
These iron accessories were
forged by the Shakers.

Fig. 11 — SHAKER BED
Mounted on large wooden casters.

sense, the first guild in America employed in manufacturing furniture on an extensive scale, and their ideals were those of the finest industrial societies of mediæval days.

Anyone who has visited the Shaker settlements has probably noted the restraint and economy with which the furniture that came from their workshops has been disposed. The aspect of purity which invariably pervades the rooms of the spacious Shaker dwellings is not accidental. These people were wont to combine the appreciation of utility with a delightful sense of arrangement, which, added to what amounted to a passion for cleanliness, produced interiors of loveliness and refinement.

Moreover, necessity mothered many an invention within the isolated communities which sprang up in New York, Massachusetts, Connecticut, New Hampshire, Maine, Ohio,

Fig. 12 — SHAKER CHEST-OF-DRAWERS
The drop leaf is a characteristic peculiarity.

Kentucky, Indiana, and Florida. Chairs and tables, for example, were often adapted to special purposes and prearranged interiors. We find such kitchen tables and chairs, dining tables and chairs, sewing tables, laundry tables, spinning chairs, children's chairs, invalids' chairs.

Because the Shakers placed chief emphasis on this utility of the products of their workshops, and because, therefore, their designs, once adopted, were perpetuated with high standards of excellence but with little subsequent artistic consciousness, their furniture has not received due appreciation. Yet there are many enthusiastic collectors of specimens of this interesting craft, who prize not only the things themselves, but also their associations with the modest folk whose spirit was transmitted to what they made as they put their "hands to work."

Fig. 1 — Settee in Cherry
The ample proportions of this piece are in keeping with the spaciousness of the Shaker rooms. Note the neatly turned knobs for holding the cording, and the massive dovetails of the frame.

The Furniture of an American Religious Sect

By Edward D. *and* Faith Andrews

Illustrations from the authors' collection

VIEWING the output of the Shaker workshops, one comes to feel, like Pope, that here is harmonious confusion, and that, "though all things differ," all agree. The wide variety of articles manufactured by this sect are so unified, both in spirit and in general plan, that their diversity is at first scarcely apparent. Yet this uniformity, this individuality, is such that Shaker pieces are as readily recognizable as examples from the great schools of furniture design.

Some acquaintance with Shaker history and beliefs is, above all, necessary to an understanding of this achieved unity. The communistic mode of life adopted by these people

Fig. 2 — Sister's Sewing Table
The many different drawer arrangements of these work tables are evidence of the individual spirit which pervaded Shaker craftsmanship. But the names of most of the artisans are forgotten.

was productive of similarities in their manners and customs, their dress, their relationships with one another and with the world. It would be strange did not their shops, from one decade to another, adhere to certain generally recognized ideas as to what constituted household appointments acceptable to the Shaker taste. For purposes of internal solidarity it was sometimes considered necessary, among other things, to issue "orders" regarding the making and finishing of furniture. Thus, at one time, in one community, all beds were to be stained a prescribed green. For a long period the practice of using a thin Venetian red or yellow ochre wash was so com-

Fig. 3 — Dutch-Foot Table (*probably early*)

An uncommon, possibly a unique example. Simple turning or tapering usually characterizes the legs of Shaker tables, though pieces were sometimes constructed with "button" feet.

Fig. 4 — Wall Table

This table has a single leaf. A drawer is available at each end. The form is an adaptation of a late eighteenth-century type. Wood, butternut, and cherry.

Fig. 5 — Tailor's Bench, from Hancock

A superior piece; all curly maple except the drop leaf. The chest was used by Shaker sisters for cutting out cloth for garments. Its movability is dependent on four small wooden casters fixed into the base of the frame. Within is a card with directions for removing the top of the bench. The instructions conclude: "This table was moved into the Elder Sisters' Room, June 22, 1843."

Size: top, 72 by 32 inches; height, 33 inches.

Fig. 6 — Shaker Stove
This stove, wrought in a Shaker forge, offers an interesting analogy to the Dutch-foot table illustrated in Figure 3. It has shaped feet, though, in most instances, the legs were short, tapering rods. A wooden model of these efficient heaters is preserved at Mt. Lebanon.

Fig. 8 — Shaker Foot Warmer

Fig. 7 (left) — Early Shaker Tilting-Chair
From the Hancock community. The detail below shows the construction at the base of the rear posts. The ball is fixed in the socket by means of a thong knotted at one end and fixed into the leg post with a wooden dowel.

mon that the name "Shaker red" or "Shaker yellow" was universally applied to these tints. The proportion of the different colors in Shaker clothes was also fixed by a holy "order." Regular hours, prearranged schedules, and fixed responsibilities were a necessary concomitant of the Shaker system. In the closely affiliated communities, countless little household processes became habitual,

passing down through the years. Shaker products became fixed in character, the common results of common folk ways.

So dominant was the religious strain in the lives of these folk that one feels that here also was a unifying force in their works. "Labor is worship and prayer," they sang. Such ideals as purity and humility were

Fig. 9 — Delicately Conceived Stands in Cherry
Note that the early, lipped drawer has given way to the later form. Native cherry, birch, butternut, pine, and maple were the woods most commonly used in Hancock and Mt. Lebanon.

Fig. 10 — Shaker Rocking-Chair; Drop Leaf Table

The chair illustrates the contention that Shakers were influenced by Colonial patterns, which often came into their homes with the reception of new members. The turning of the legs of the little table is characteristic. The drawer is unusually narrow. Wood, cherry throughout.

Fig. 11 — Desk on Tripod Base; Two Sewing Stands

As far as can be discovered, the desk is a unique piece. The pedestal is curly maple, the desk itself, butternut. Whether the drawers on these sewing stands are original, or are later additions, is undetermined. Several such stands exist, a fact which favors the first alternative. Note the fine dovetailing of the drawers. These pieces are apparently derivatives of Colonial stands.

transferred into what they wrought, transmitting to it a highly individual quality—chaste, unassuming, almost spiritual.

In the latter quarter of the nineteenth century, with the issuance of patents and the subsequent development of chairmaking for commercial purposes — especially at Mount Lebanon and Harvard — an inevitable standardization took place, resulting in a product quite distinctive and widely known.* Popular interest in this community craftsmanship might soon have waned, however, if its authors had been hampered by unduly rigid, semi-ecclesiastic ideas of conformity. As a matter of fact, individual development was encouraged. The little groups were strengthened by assigning to each member the work that he or she was best fitted to perform, and then by permitting a free activity in the performance. Further, as their occupational history abundantly shows, the Shakers were a practical-minded people. Their material success was due in large measure so their dogma of doing everything as efficiently as possible.

A long list of inventions bears evidence to the scientific management of the Shaker farms, industries, and homes. Agricultural, industrial, and domestic thoroughness was a daily duty and habit. Here lies the explanation of that wide variety of forms which is the delight of the lover of Shaker furniture. Pieces were made on definite order, their function foreseen, but with no concessions to unloveliness. The diverse demands

* Shaker chairs and stools were distributed in the Middle West, mainly through the agency of the Marshall Field Company of Chicago. They have long been popular in New England.

Fig. 12 — A Shaker Tall Clock (1806)

Little is known of Benjamin Youngs, save that he labored in the early Watervliet settlement. He is said to have been the nephew of that Benjamin Youngs of wider note, co-author of *Christ's First and Second Appearing (1808)*, who, at the time when this clock was made, was serving on the important mission which established Shaker societies in Ohio and Kentucky. The date, *1806*, is probably correct, though crayoned later. Youngs also made wall clocks. The wood is cherry.

of large households were met, not only by scores of ingenious labor-saving devices, but by a multiform furniture, each piece of which directly related to a recognized need.

This does not imply that variety was never sought for its own sake, or that of the intrinsic beauty of the product. Many of the Shaker cabinetmakers were artists, for whom form rather than function held the larger meaning. For a prosperous half century or more after 1820, an era in which the Shakers were largely independent of the world, it is not strange that a profession of cabinetmakers, working freely and industriously at the task of adapting beauty to use, should have turned out an amazing assortment of "sprightly" pieces. Exceptional personalities, men of the skill of James Farnum, Gilbert Avery, John Lockwood, George Wickersham, Benjamin Youngs, Thomas Fisher, and Robert Wagan, attuned to the Shaker spirit of simplicity, designed and executed hundreds of unpretentious pieces. These, in turn, were copied by apprentices, or were altered to fit particular needs. For nearly a century, however, the craft was characterized by a vitality which was naturally productive of rich diversity.

It is unfortunate that lack of space prevents the use of enough illustrations to make this "order in variety" self-evident. Perhaps the few selected, along with those previously published,* will sufficiently indicate the restrained charm and sound workmanship which resides in even the commonest of Shaker pieces.

* See ANTIQUES, Vol. XIV, page 132.

An Interpretation of Shaker Furniture

By EDWARD D. AND FAITH ANDREWS

Illustrations, except as noted, from the authors' collection

"To me more dear, congenial to my heart
One native charm, than all the gloss of art."
— Oliver Goldsmith, *The Deserted Village*

Fig. 1 — SWIVEL SEWING CHAIR
A Shaker derivative of the Windsor type. Chiefly of maple

Fig. 2 — SHAKER CHAIR
Ironing chair with seat twenty inches above the floor

IN THE program of the early Shakers, little place was left for the intentional cultivation of beauty. Not only did the practical aspects of making a livelihood lead to neglect of the decorative arts, but the tenets of the Believers were so interpreted that the beautiful was considered unnecessary to the highest life, and therefore wrong. Thus Elder Frederick Evans, one of Shakerdom's chief spokesmen, is quoted as stating, "The beautiful . . . has no business with us. The divine man has no right to waste money upon what you people would call beauty, in his house or his daily life, while there are people living in misery." (*The Communistic Societies of the United States*, Charles Nordhoff, *1875*.) If he were to build his dwellings and shops again, he would aim, not to make them more beautiful, but to assure more light, a better distribution of heat, and a more inclusive regard for protection and comfort, because such concerns promote health and long life — a basally functional point of view. The members of the sect have always been known as "strict utilitarians." In a book entitled *Two Years' Experience among the Shakers* (*1848*) a certain David Lamson writes: "In all they do, the first inquiry is, will it be useful? Everything therefore about their buildings, fences, etc. is plain."

In this attitude the Shakers differed little from other communal societies in this country. Only the Harmonists, who were taught by Father Rapp to love music and flowers, and the Oneida Perfectionists, who fostered musical and theatrical entertainments and landscape gardening, appear to have encouraged the æsthetic side of existence.

The utilitarian conception voiced by Elder Evans strongly influenced the furniture craft among the Shakers. The necessary relationship between utility and sound workmanship was obvious. Shaker furniture was always fashioned in the spirit of Mother Ann's injunction: "Do your work as if you had a thousand years to live and as if you were to die tomorrow." The same care that was expended on chests, tables, chairs, and beds was lavished on workbenches, broom vises, shoe benches and racks, sanding machine frames, and the trays for carrying berry baskets from the field. Moreover, everything had to be plain in aspect, not only because all ornament or embellishment was believed to be wrong, but because, as ardent disciples of cleanliness, the Shakers knew that the simpler a piece was, the more easily could it be kept unsoiled.

The character of Shaker furniture was in no small measure determined by the fact that each item was utilized in the immediate community where it was made. Thus the general household requirement was often modified by the particular need of the individual. The purpose that a given piece was to serve, and even the place where it would stand, were known to the maker, and tended to emphasize the functionality of the finished work.

Fig. 3 — SHAKER CHAIRS
a. Child's chair. *Height: 11 inches to seat, 24 inches to topmost slat. b.* Adult's rocker. The bar across the top is to permit application of an upholstered back. *Height: 43 inches to cushion rail*

This accounts in part for the large number of unduplicated pieces that has come to light. Committed though they were to independence from worldly sources of supply, the Shakers could not prevent the element of variability from entering into the production of their shops. They had to turn out not only such essential pieces of furniture as tables, chairs, chests of drawers, and beds, but countless accessory forms, such as clocks, bookcases, washstands, soap boxes, sinks, knife boxes, brushes, brooms, trunks, benches, mirror frames, stools, foot warmers, wood boxes, measuring sticks, sewing boxes, dust boxes, mixing bowls, bean boxes, squash squeezers, foot measures, letter boxes, trays, pincushion holders, coffins, counters, tailoring benches, and so on. The Shaker cabinet-maker, obviously, was forced to be unusually versatile.

Unless, however, one grants to the craftsman some very clear appreciation of the beautiful for its

Fig. 4 — HIGH WORK BENCH
Made especially to support three mixing bowls for preparing white, graham, and unleavened bread. Omission of braces in front permits worker to sit at his task

Fig. 5 — SHAKER STOOLS
The two-step stools were equally useful as foot rests and as portable steps. They are exclusively Shaker. The legs of the tripod stool are characteristic

own sake, it is difficult to explain how Shaker craftsmanship so long maintained its excellence. Its inherent æsthetic quality must have won a degree of recognition that helped to maintain the tradition of good workmanship and supplied inspiration for some of the fine pieces constructed during the midyears of the last century. Though even as late as the 'seventies and 'eighties

Elder Evans and other leaders officially repudiated "beauty," evidences of a more liberal conception of the place of the arts in a desirable community life are not lacking.

A reaction had set in against the constraints that accompanied the revivalistic ardors of the founders. The natural desire of newcomers, especially young people, to enjoy some gratification of the senses also had its slow effect. Flowers, for instance, came to be appreciated for their color and fragrance as well as for their value in the making of extracts and medicines. By the early 'seventies a Shaker Elder, Giles B. Avery, proclaimed that "Creative Providence made flowers beautiful, and made the eye with capacity to drink in their beauty, to contribute to the happiness of His creatures." Music and poetry also advanced beyond their strictly religious function to play a part in a gradually increasing, though always limited, recreational life. During the last half of the nineteenth century several volumes of poetry were published, while *The Shaker* — the official monthly publication of the sect — as well as its successor, *The Manifesto*, printed words and scores of many hymns and songs.

The Shaker author of the book *The Aletheia* went so far as to predict that "the arts as well as the sciences would some day

Fig. 6 — SMALL SEWING "DESK" OR CABINET
Of maple and cherry, painted Shaker red. Unusual because of size

Fig. 7 — BUREAU DESK
A Shaker version of a type of desk that was much in vogue at the beginning of the nineteenth century

flourish under the patronage of those living the highest life, the Shaker life"; and Hinds, in his *American Communities (1902)*, noted that "there is a growing party of progressives, who, while firmly adhering to all the essentials of Shakerism, demand that non-essentials shall not stand in the way of genuine progress and culture."

But the best of Shaker furniture had been made before this conscious broadening of culture. All the more reason for praising the early cabinet-

Fig. 8 (right) — SMALL CHEST OF DRAWERS Of butternut. The brasses are a recent substitution for original Shaker knobs. *Size: 25 ¾ inches high by 24 ½ inches wide. From the collection of Mrs. Carl de Gersdorff*

Fig. 10 (below) — PINE CASE WITH DRAWERS AND CUPBOARDS Fine paneling distinguishes early Shaker work such as this. Best examples are found on doors and window casings of meetinghouses. In the piece illustrated, the doors spring open when pressure is applied to protruding wrought-iron pins

Fig. 9 (above, right) — PINE CHEST OF DRAWERS
Marked *Lucy Bishop's Case. Made by A. B. April 3, 1817.* The initials stand for Amos Bishop, an early cabinetmaker of the Mount Lebanon community. In general, the piece follows late eighteenth-century precedent
Fig. 11 (below, right) — PINE CUPBOARD. Unique and apparently quite early

makers who anticipated the subsequent attitude and, in an atmosphere of apparent indifference to any consideration but that of utility, created and maintained a school of design which later won honor. The conventions that kept their work simple in character could not bind their imaginations, but, on the contrary, gave purity and direction to their skill.

In the early days of the Shaker communities no pieces of furniture were more widely in use than benches. Constructed in heavy native pine, sometimes with basswood tops, they were a frequent substitute for chairs. Deal benches ten feet long, or longer, were placed in the dining and meeting rooms. Shorter forms, sometimes equipped with a drawer, were used as spinning stools, for holding flowerpots, keeping sundry containers above basement floors, supporting coffins, and so on. One of these benches is shown in Figure 4. It has a medial brace tightly keyed on the outside of the leg, somewhat in the manner of Swedish refectory tables. The braces are dovetailed, and the vertical members are mortised, Windsor fashion, into the top. The two-step stools (*Fig. 5*), designed as foot rests, and the "three-steppers," used to reach tall chests of drawers and sometimes equipped with a

— small chests, cupboards, table desks, wall racks, and so on, which show that the producers recognized the convenience of appurtenances. It is true that members of the sect were amply provided with efficiently designed furniture and tools that lightened the daily tasks — even though the emphasis was always on usefulness and durability, and no concessions were made to what the Shakers believed was the human weakness for vulgar display. In the items that have been selected to illustrate this study, we perceive constant evidence that æsthetic satisfaction accompanied the creative effort. And

Fig. 12 (above) — WORK TABLE
Interesting and convenient disposition of drawers

Fig. 13 (right) — RARE STRETCHER TABLE
An exceptionally dignified piece. Originally an ironing table, later used for canning. Top strengthened by addition of strips under the edges. On the table are a small hanging cupboard and a dovetailed chest

supporting rod or rods for the hand, belong in the same category. Strength is their outstanding characteristic; but they are a delight to behold, especially when covered with the soft-hued mat work from the sewing rooms of the Sisters.

The passion for utility among Shaker cabinet-makers is nowhere better illustrated than in the high pine chests (*Fig. 10*) which were used for nearly every room in dwelling house or shop. Often they were built into the wall structure; sometimes, as in this case, they stood out from the walls and were equipped with cupboard space. Though of generous dimensions, rising on occasion almost to the ceiling, they never seem ungainly or ill-proportioned. The paneling of the cupboard doors is finely achieved, the knobs are delicately turned, and the total effect is one of chaste perfection. In contrast to this chest is the small butternut stand pictured in Figure 8, a diminutive bureau of most charming quality. Many such pieces have come to light

we are glad that strict limitations defined the character of the work, for, in the instinctive and perhaps unconscious evasion of the prescriptive letter, the free spirit of the craftsman has become unfailingly manifest.

Fig. 16 (above) — PAN CUPBOARD
On the wall above is a hanging rack

Figs. 14 and 15 (left) — TWO UNUSUAL STANDS
(*early*)
For convenience the former stand has a tilted top and the height is adjustable

75

SHAKER SIMPLICITY
A Photographic Study by W. F. Winter, from the
collection of Mr. and Mrs. Edward Deming Andrews

Antiques in
Domestic Settings

Solutions and Suggestions

XIII. Shaker Home of Mr. and Mrs. Edward Deming
Andrews in Pittsfield, Massachusetts

THE word functionalism was probably quite outside the vocabulary of Shakerdom. But what was "practical" and what was not, the Shakers understood better than most of their worldly neighbors. Untroubled by philosophies of style, they nevertheless held to a very clear philosophy of craftsmanship. Whatsoever they built must serve a useful purpose;

Dining Room in the Shaker Mode (*above*)
    All the furniture is from New York and New England Shaker communities, where it was made. Pewter, glass, and other ware, though of outside manufacture, were acquired from Shaker establishments

Another View of the Dining Room (*right*)
    Note the peg rail along the wall at a convenient height above the floor, and the manner in which the hanging shelves are fitted to it. The capacious chest of drawers is from a Shaker workroom. The Shakers made tinware, and did not a little work in casting and forging iron. For glass, pottery, and pewter they appear to have depended upon worldly sources of supply

it must be in so far as possible perfectly constructed, and it must be devoid of all decorative embellishment. In the upshot, this meant that Shaker dwellings and Shaker furniture represented a virtually unconscious response to current styles and canons of proportion, which were in turn very consciously reduced to the ultimate of simplicity and subjected to further modification to meet the stern demands of utility.

To Shaker furniture as it may be studied in individual examples ANTIQUES has in the past devoted considerable attention. Never before, however, has opportunity been afforded to illustrate the employment of such furniture in a present-day domestic setting carefully and intelligently devised to bring the traditional Shaker modes within the compass of today's family need and convenience.

The views here presented are from the dining room and a bedroom in the home of Mr. and Mrs. Edward D. Andrews of Pittsfield, Massachusetts, who have won recognition as authorities in the domain of Shaker arts and crafts and the beliefs and customs by which these manifestations were inspired.

It should perhaps be remarked that, in accordance with Shaker prescription, the walls of the dining room are white, the woodwork a delightful grayish blue, the plain curtains white, and the furniture in native hues

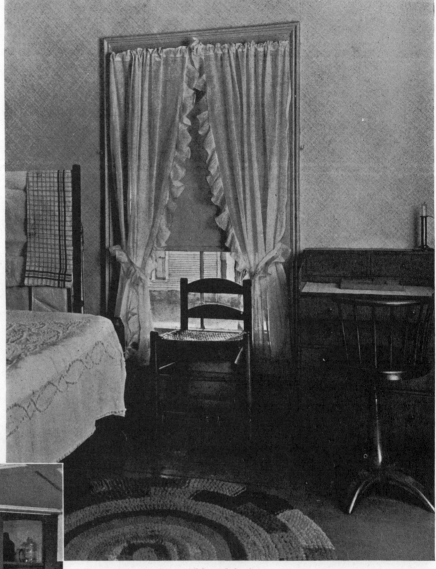

BEDROOM IN THE SHAKER MODE (*above*)
Simplicity coupled with extraordinary purity of line and perfection of finish gives Shaker furniture an air of demure yet affecting distinction. The swivel chair is indicative of Shaker progressiveness. Observe, too, the conveniently large wheels on the bedstead legs

ANOTHER VIEW OF THE DINING ROOM (*left*)
The corner cupboard, painted blue to match the rest of the wood trim, is a characteristic Shaker piece. The deep-aproned table with raked legs is an exceptionally good example of Shaker design. Chairs like the two pictured not only were used by the Shakers but found a ready market throughout the country

of pine, walnut, birch, and maple ripened and enriched by time.

Allowances must be made for the fact that in the quarters thus converted to an earlier faith some ineradicable features of late architectural heathenism were perforce retained. Mr. and Mrs. Andrews hope that some day they may build or adapt a veritable Shaker dwelling undefiled by worldling ideas of design, and that thay may equip the place throughout with the best of old Shaker furniture. Such an ambition is deserving of fulfilment, for it points toward something far more significant than an archæological reconstruction. Its true intent is to demonstrate the unimpaired validity of Shaker patterns and their adaptability to a modern design for worthy and unaffected living.

For photographs ANTIQUES is indebted to the skill and understanding of Vicentini-Herrich and to the very special courtesy of the Art Service Project of the Federal Government.

DOORWAY TO QUIETUDE

Kitchen of the Shaker-furnished home of Doctor and Mrs. Edward Deming Andrews. The quiet dignity of these utilitarian pieces of furniture, and the rectilinear simplicity of their background, offer satisfaction to the eye and repose to the spirit. Other rooms in the Andrews house are illustrated elsewhere in this issue. *Photograph by William F. Winter*

Unusual forms in Shaker furniture

BY E. RAY PEARSON, *Associate professor, Institute of Design, Illinois Institute of Technology*

and HINMAN L. P. KEALY, *Associate professor of architecture, University of Illinois*

NO INDIVIDUAL OR GROUP creates in a vacuum, or evolves an aesthetic philosophy without contact with contemporary events. The work of the Shakers clearly reflects this fact. All of their original furniture and implements were brought to the communities as contributions of the converts. There is, for example, in the collection of the Fruitlands Museum at Harvard, Massachusetts, a simple turned windsor chair which reputedly was used by Mother Ann. This chair, although converted to a rocker, is typical of those made in

Fig. 1. Bentwood chair with web seat and back, from Mount Lebanon, c. 1880. The splaying of the front legs and the thinning at the curve of the shaped arm and the top of the back are particularly notable. *Hancock Shaker Village; except as noted, photographs are by E. Ray Pearson.*

Fig. 2. Oak secretary made by Elder Henry Green of Alfred, c. 1884.
Collection of the Sabbathday Lake Shakers.

Fig. 3. Gold decalcomania label, 1½ by 2 inches. These were printed in large sheets and cut out by hand. Printer's mark PF & Co., N.Y. P 3836 for Palm Fechteler & Co., of New York and Chicago, on reverse. *Privately owned.*

Fig. 4. Two sisters' sewing desks of mixed woods; note tops shaped to fit together. *Sabbathday Lake collection.*

rural New England during the eighteenth century.

The furniture which the Shakers themselves designed quite often reflected the more complicated tastes of the Victorian era, or the technical improvements of the mid-nineteenth century. For example, while the Shakers had used bentwood earlier, it was not until the introduction of Thonet's furniture at the Philadelphia Exhibition of 1876, at which they also showed their chairs, that the Shakers effectively combined so few components into a satisfactory whole. Figure 1 reveals the influence of the work of Thonet in the use of a single piece of shaped wood outlining the back and forming the rear legs of the chair, and front legs and arms made of two additional shaped and bent pieces. The secretary in Figure 2 is also clearly related to "worldly" design of its era.

The Shakers had manufactured furniture, particularly chairs, for sale as early as the 1790's. In the 1870's they were mass producing a sufficient number of chairs and foot benches to justify the issuance of catalogues. This production lasted until 1947, when Eldress Sarah Collins of Mount Lebanon terminated it. Genuine Shaker chairs bore trade-mark labels (Fig. 3), and the Shakers warned against

imitations. The Mount Lebanon catalogue of 1875 told buyers to

Look for our trade mark before purchasing—no chair is genuine without it. Our trade mark is a gold transfer, and is designed to be ornamental; but, if objectionable to purchasers, it can be easily removed without defacing the furniture in the least, by wetting a sponge or piece of cotton cloth with aqua ammonia and rubbing it until it is loosened.

The Shakers on the whole lived in a rustic world, so it is surprising to find many subtle refinements in their furniture. Perhaps this is explained by two factors: many of the leaders were accomplished craftsmen, and the society, while communal, emphasized the individual's productive role. The latter point is particularly important, for one cannot be at one's most productive if one is physically uncomfortable; hence the tremendous variety of adjustments made to standard items. It is further important to remember that any major changes were theoretically approved by the central ministry at Mount Lebanon, which tended to give a homogeneous quality to early Shaker designs. This can be verified in the many journals surviving at the Western Reserve Historical Society Library and the Shaker Museums at Old

Fig. 5. Writing desk on stand (two views);
date and community unknown.
Collection of Mr. and Mrs. H. L. Lurie.

Fig. 6. Two-piece double secretary from Shirley;
date unknown. The paint is not original.
Privately owned.

Fig. 7. Two-piece walnut secretary, or plantation desk, with drawer in base unit and original leather writing surface; date unknown, but undoubtedly post-Civil War. South Union. *Collection of Mrs. Curry Churchill Hall.*

Fig. 8. Two "dwarf tall case alarm clocks," made by Benjamin S. Youngs, Watervliet, New York. *Left:* c. 1800; height 36⅞ inches. *Right:* c. 1812; height 36⅛ inches. *Henry Ford Museum.*

Chatham, New York, and Canterbury, New Hampshire, or in other collections.

On the other hand, there was great variation in the types of production in the different communities. Each was self-supporting and strove to develop products which would guarantee its independence. At least three communities in Ohio and Kentucky (particularly South Union, Kentucky) specialized in silk production. Silk dyeing and weaving required equipment considerably different from that used by the Sabbathday Lake group in their manufacture of water-proof cloth. There was a general pattern for sewing table-desks, but this pattern could be and was frequently adjusted to suit the convenience and the physical characteristics of the individual sister who was to use the piece. In the hand-some pair shown in Figure 4 the over-all dimensions are identical, but the drawer arrangements are not.

The maintenance of ledgers, journals, and diaries was an integral part of the activity of each community, so writing tables provide some of the best examples of adaptation of pieces of furniture throughout the years. Reference has been made to the rather late secretary in Figure 2; a fine early example is the writing table in Figure 5. In essence, this is an eighteenth-century traveling desk to which has been

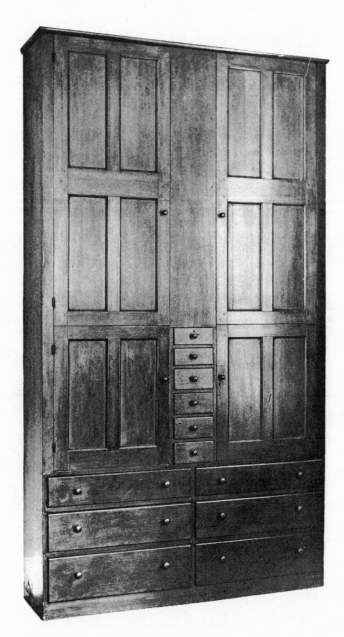

floor. An exceptional example of this freestanding type is illustrated in Figure 9. What is most unusual here is the series of six small drawers in the center panel. There are shelves behind the hinged doors.

Another interesting storage piece is the small chest in Figure 10. Although it is simply constructed, its subtle proportions give it a certain elegance. The extremely thick top, straight sides forming solid legs, and the open space between clearly indicate that this was used in one of the shops.

As the Shakers gradually closed their communities, the movable contents of their buildings might be distributed to friends, sold at auction, or transferred to still-operating communities. The Kentucky Building at Western Kentucky University in Bowling Green has several Shaker items which passed into private hands as gifts. What is surprising is the vast amount of furniture which survives. In part, of course, the solid Shaker construction accounts for this. "Do your work," Mother Ann had said, "as if you had a thousand years to live, and as if you were to die tomorrow." Elder Blinn refers to some dining chairs made in 1834 by Elder Micajah Tucker which were still in use and in good repair in 1892. This set had the lightness characteristic of Shaker liftable pieces.

Many of the pieces cannot be accurately dated or attributed to any particular maker or locale. Only buildings were dated. With Shaker furniture, dating must be based on stylistic elements which changed with the changing tastes of the people from whom the Shakers were converted and with whom they maintained percipient contact.

added a base with a drawer and arms to support the writing surface when it is opened. As the activities of the society became more complex larger units were needed, and some were made wide enough to accommodate two writers (Fig. 6). A fourth variation, reflecting local influence, is the plantation-style desk (Fig. 7). In the size and division of its compartments it is a typical nineteenth-century Southern piece, yet the turnings and other details are characteristic of the work of the Western Shakers.

In the earlier periods only a few of the leaders had timepieces, and the community relied on bells. Soon, however, the usefulness of clocks was recognized, and they were installed in every dwelling and many of the shops. They were of several types, including grandfather, grandmother, and wall clocks. Two interesting examples are the dwarf alarm clocks in the Henry Ford Museum (Fig. 8), made by an early convert.

Many people associate sizable built-in cupboards and chests with the Shakers; often, however, these large pieces were freestanding, although they might be flush with the

Regional characteristics of Western Shaker furniture

BY JULIA NEAL, *Director, Kentucky Library and Museum, Western Kentucky University*

THE EARLIEST FURNITURE used by the Shakers in Kentucky and Ohio is in the clean-lined and functional style of the Eastern Shaker furniture. The Western craftsmen knew well the precepts taught by the first leaders relating to the making of furniture, but it was not the Millennial Laws prohibiting decorative trim that prevented the embellishment of these pieces so much as it was the pressing need to provide the essential equipment for mushrooming memberships. At South Union, for example, in the two decades between 1807 and 1827 the membership rose from 26 to 349. Building large dwelling houses as well as the necessary workshops and providing all of these with adequate furniture left little time for superfluities.

The case of drawers (Fig. 1) from the Watervliet, Ohio, society is a classic example of early Shaker design. Two large bottom drawers and twenty-one smaller ones arranged three to a row permit easy and orderly storing of objects of varying size. The chest also sits flat on the floor, after the fashion of Eastern case pieces.

Also made along Eastern Shaker lines is the ladder-back chair with woven-tape seat, shaped slats, and familiar finials

(Fig. 2). A variant slat was widely used on Western chairs (Fig. 3).

Benches, instead of chairs, were used at first in meeting rooms and the meetinghouse as well as in dining rooms. A simple Kentucky bench (Fig. 4) was made of only four pieces. It could be taken apart easily, since each end was mortised into a stretcher under the seat and had two square tenons mortised through the top board, flush with the surface.

Dining-room benches were eventually replaced by the one-slat or two-slat chair (Fig. 4). The change was hailed by a South Union journalist: "Jan. 1, 1849—*Chairs for the Dining tables*—Brethren on this Blessed New Years Day begin to make chairs for the dining room and so get clear of the benches."

A more sophisticated Kentucky chair (Fig. 5) came later. It had a solid wooden seat, some turnings, and "mule-ear" posts. Spindles replaced the second slat. All the early dining chairs were low enough to slip under the tables when not in use, which made for orderliness. Much later a taller and more refined chair, with two slats and delicate vertical

Fig. 1. Case of drawers made at Watervliet, Ohio. Height 60 inches. *Collection of Mr. and Mrs. Robert H. Jones.* Cherry desk with maple drawers, made at Union Village, Ohio. Height 36 inches. *Warren County (Ohio) Historical Society; photograph by A. J. Wyatt, courtesy of the Philadelphia Museum of Art.*

Fig. 2. Ladder-back chair,
painted Shaker red.
Height 38½ inches.
*Shakertown
(Pleasant Hill, Kentucky);
photograph by
H. J. Scheirich III.*

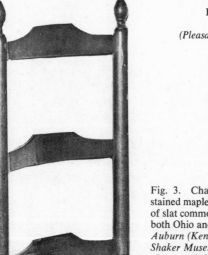

Fig. 3. Chair back of
stained maple with type
of slat common in
both Ohio and Kentucky.
*Auburn (Kentucky)
Shaker Museum;
photograph by
Kalman Papp.*

spindles, was made at Pleasant Hill (see ANTIQUES, November 1947, p. 356).

It is not surprising that the Kentucky and Ohio Shakers, who were culturally deeply rooted in Virginia, North Carolina, and Pennsylvania, came more and more to use designs with which they had long been familiar. The fact that the Easterners were beginning to vary their own early patterns made it easier for the Western artisans to modify the traditional forms.

The Western Shakers made early use of the turned leg rather than the plain tapered one. The pronounced turnings of a South Union example (Fig. 6) are obviously intended to be decorative rather than functional.

The South Union Church Family lived in what had been the home of Jesse McComb, the second convert in that Kentucky society. In 1814 McComb made a chest of drawers (Fig. 7) which, following the early Shaker pattern, had numerous graduated drawers, each with its round flat wooden knob; the turned feet that lift the chest six inches from the floor are more Southern than Shaker.

Another example of variation which can be called Southern embellishment is the ogee molding used on an otherwise simple kitchen piece (Fig. 8); however, the porcelain knobs and the brass hinges and lock remain within the Eastern Shaker tradition. Since the society carpenters always knew where a piece would be located, it is probable that in this kitchen press, the need for passing room was felt to justify the awkwardness of the dropped leaf's blocking the bottom doors.

The early use of a non-functional scrolled skirt is to be seen on the lower part of an 1827 chest of drawers (Fig. 9) from Union Village. Another decorative device which served no real purpose is the rounded, scroll-like piece added to the headboard of an early Kentucky bed (Fig. 10). It fits onto the headboard by means of a deep groove and can be removed, indicating that it was a late addition. In fact, the later the piece the more evidence there is of departure from the earlier Shaker forms. It is easy to tell which of the three South Union sewing tables (Figs. 11, 13, 14) is the earliest. Although they vary in style from plain to fancy, each piece has been made on the Shaker principle of functionalism.

At least one distinctive Western Shaker form seems to have emerged from the Southern furniture tradition: the two-piece Shaker press, consisting of a cabinet on a separate base. Considerable variety in size and style exists among such presses (Figs. 15, 16).

American Midwestern traits also influenced Western Shaker furniture. One example is the pierced tin panels of the food safe in Figure 4. Another is the finish on a blanket chest from Union Village (Fig. 12) on which two layers of paint or varnish, or both—one light, the other dark—were applied. A patterned effect was achieved by drawing a comblike instrument across the surface before the second coat was thoroughly dry.

Kentucky and Ohio craftsmen also achieved decorative effects by contrasting two or more woods of different colors. A thin maple bead has been used effectively around the bottom drawer of the Kentucky cherry press in Figure 16. A bolder contrast is found on the Ohio desk of Figure 1, where maple drawers stand out against the cherry of the rest of the piece.

A rich variety of woods was available to Western Shakers. Cherry, black walnut, white walnut or butternut, maple, ash, pine, poplar, and various types of oak were all abundant. Cherry and walnut, prized by the artisans, were almost

Fig. 4. Pieces from South Union, Kentucky. Walnut bench; length 58 inches. Trestle table with walnut top, white-ash base; length 106 inches; top made of 13 strips doweled together. Two-slat maple chair with split-hickory bottom; height to top of post, 24¼ inches. Food safe, walnut with tin panels pierced for ventilation in handsome patterns; painted red; height 87 inches. *Auburn Shaker Museum; photograph by Tommy Hughes.*

Fig. 5. Dining-room chair
from Pleasant Hill;
natural finish.
Height 27¼ inches.
*Shakertown;
Scheirich photograph.*

Fig. 6. South Union cherry table. Height 29¾ inches.
*Kentucky Building, Western Kentucky University;
photograph by E. Ray Pearson.*

87

Fig. 7. South Union chest,
stained cherry wood; 1814.
Height 56 inches.
Auburn Shaker Museum; Papp Photograph.

Fig. 8. South Union early walnut cupboard
with yellow-poplar shelves.
Solid sides with cutouts forming feet;
molding with center flute
and ogee on either side. Height 79 inches.
Western Kentucky University; Papp photograph.

Fig. 9. White-walnut chest of drawers from Union Village.
Signed and dated *1827*. Height 52 inches.
Warren County Historical Society Museum;
Pearson photograph.

always used for the better pieces, such as a cherry candle-stand for the meetinghouse or a walnut trestle table for the ministry's dining room. Since all of these were plentiful, more ordinary furniture was sometimes made of the better woods too.

Kentucky and Ohio Shaker furniture, like that of the East, was finished in several ways. Cherry and walnut pieces were usually left with a natural finish. Sometimes pieces made from such woods as poplar or pine were stained or painted; red and blue seem to have been used more often than the Shaker mustard.

Little if any Shaker furniture was made in Kentucky and Ohio after the 1870's. Here furniture was made to accommodate the members, not to be sold as it was in the East. After 1870 there was little need for any additional furniture because the enrollment at all of the Ohio and Kentucky colonies began to fall off sharply. In 1889 North Union closed, and in 1922 South Union. Between these dates all the other Western societies disbanded.

Fig. 12.   Blanket chest, walnut, from Union Village. Length 50½ inches. *Warren County Historical Society; Pearson photograph.*

Fig. 13.   Cherry sewing table with splayed legs, from South Union. Cutting board beneath drawer. Lift, or rise, at back of top has wallpapered panels and red leather strips marked into sections by brass buttons forming places for keeping scissors, thimble, etc. *Auburn Shaker Museum; Papp photograph.*

Fig. 14.   South Union sewing table; cherry body, maple top rails. Only 22¾ inches high, this was used by Sister Angeline Perryman, who was small in stature. *Western Kentucky University; photograph by Arvid Van Dyke.*

Fig. 15.   Two-unit press from South Union.
Cherry with maple trim; one shelf.
Height 46½ inches.
Auburn Shaker Museum; Papp photograph.

Fig. 16.   Another two-unit press, also from South Union.
Cherry; two shelves. Put together with dowels.
Height 53¾ inches. *Papp photograph.*

The Shaker furniture of Elder Henry Green

BY MARY GRACE CARPENTER AND CHARLES H. CARPENTER JR.

ELDER HENRY GREEN, one of the last great Shaker crafts-men, joined the Shakers at Alfred, Maine, as a boy of fifteen in 1859. He lived at that community until it closed in the spring of 1931 and then, along with the remaining twenty-one members of the Alfred community, moved to the Sabbathday Lake, Maine, community where he died on September 5, 1931. Henry Green served his community as a cabinetmaker, carpenter, school teacher, purchasing agent, salesman, commercial manager, and finally, for more than thirty years, as the spiritual leader of the Shakers at Alfred.

Although a devout Shaker, Henry Green had many contacts with the outside world. He was a long-time ac-quaintance and friend of many well-known New Englanders of his time. His literary friends included Kate Douglas Wiggin,[1] William Dean Howells, Sarah Orne Jewett, Mar-garet Deland,[2] and John Greenleaf Whittier.

That he will be remembered primarily for his furniture would probably have struck Henry Green as ironic. Cabi-netmaking was a major occupation for him only between approximately 1870 and 1890, and almost all his furniture was made for the Shakers' own use, rather than for sale. Green's apprenticeship as a cabinetmaker started under Elder Joshua Bussell probably almost immediately after he came to Alfred in 1859. At this time the Shakers were at their peak numerically and the ideals of usefulness and simplicity were still followed by Shaker craftsmen. The Civil War was a watershed for the movement. In the turmoil that followed it, enrollment in the Shaker communities began its long decline, while the industrialization of the Reconstruction era made it more economical for the Shakers to buy much of the furniture they had previously made. Henry Green's career spanned this decline of Sha-kerism. By 1890, when furniture making ceased to be Green's chief occupation, many Shaker communities were faced with the problem of vacant buildings and a surplus of most kinds of furniture.

During the 1870's Henry Green made for the Alfred community sewing desks, tailor's bunks, looms, and a cheese press. Although they are all characteristically Shaker in form and construction they display a greater use of contrasting paints and stains and a greater variety of woods than was typical at the Shaker community in Mount Leb-anon, New York.

Fig. 1.   Matched pair of sewing desks, made by Elder Henry Green (1844-1931) at Alfred, Maine, c. 1875. The drawer fronts are oak, frames maple, and panels birch. Over-all height 35½, width 26, depth 20½ inches. *Except as noted, illustrations are from the Shaker Museum, Sabbathday Lake, Maine, and photographs are by David W. Serette.*

Pl. I. Sewing desk, made by Green at Alfred, c. 1875. The frame is maple, the panels pine, the drawer fronts butternut, and the knobs cherry. Frame and panels have a thin wash of red paint. Height 40¼, width 30¼, depth 24⅜ inches. *Private collection; photograph by Alan Mitchell.*

Pl. II. Secretary, made by Green at Alfred, c. 1882. It was used to keep the ministry records at Alfred. Woods are maple and butternut. Height 83, width 40½, depth 20 inches.

The Maine Shakers from the beginning made greater use of color and contrasting woods to cheer up households and shops during the long and often bleak winters. Floors were painted pumpkin yellow; furniture was finished in soft shades of red, yellow, and sometimes blue. Bird's-eye maple was used alone or with darker woods, and drawer fronts of maple or birch or butternut were set in frames of cherry or other woods which had been stained dark red.

The sewing desk or table, of which Henry Green made more than a dozen during the 1870's, was a characteristic form of the Maine and New Hampshire Shakers,[3] although examples have been found in other communities.[4] Green's mentor, Elder Joshua Bussell, is known to have made at least one sewing desk at Alfred before the Civil War. It is boxy in shape and the cabinetwork, particularly in the interior, is somewhat crude, but the design of a bank of small drawers mounted on top and at the back of a chest of drawers with a pull-out slide probably served as a guide to Henry Green. Green's fine desks were the culmination of the form and the best of them rank with the best Shaker furniture ever made. The perfect proportions and the happy combination of light butternut drawer fronts and red frame in the little desk shown in Plate I are the work of a master craftsman.

Fig. 2.   Tailor's bunk or bench, made by Green at Alfred, c. 1875. The top is pine, the frame maple, the drawer fronts oak, and the pulls cherry. Height 35¼, length 71, depth 33¾ inches.

Fig. 3.   Two-harness loom, made by Green at Alfred, c. 1875. It was used for weaving straw, narrow braid, or tapes. Woods are maple and oak. Height 61 inches.

With the exception of the miniature matched pair shown in Figure 1, Green's sewing desks differ slightly from each other in detail and proportion. The backs of all of them are paneled in the same manner as the sides, allowing them to be used either against a wall or freestanding in a room. The white porcelain knobs on their cutting boards appear to be original.

The five other known examples of Henry Green's early cabinetwork are a large worktable or tailor's bunk (Fig. 2), three looms, one of which is shown in Figure 3, and a cheese press (Fig. 4). Like his early sewing desks, these pieces show Green working in the Maine Shaker tradition. They have the reticence and simplicity of the best Shaker furniture of the preceding fifty years.

Some, but not all, of the furniture Green made in the 1880's took a Victorian turn. A dozen or so writing desks decorated with scrollwork which he made for the sisters, for example (see Fig. 5), are a far cry from the sewing desks of only a few years earlier. Despite their simple drawer fronts and the plain, paneled drop lid, the writing desks have lost their Shaker look. But Henry Green's Shaker contemporaries liked them. Elder Otis Sawyer wrote of them in 1883: "Brother Henry Green made three very nice writing desks, two of which were for the Ministry Sisters and [one for] Eldress Eliza Smith. They contain four larger and [inside] two small drawers a folding leaf, partings for paper and on top two shelves for books."[5]

A brief review of the history of the Alfred community and Henry Green's life during the 1870's and 1880's will help to explain why some of Green's furniture drifted away from the Shaker models of the past.[6] A sharp decline in the quality of rural life in Maine after the Civil War caused both the Alfred and Sabbathday Lake Shaker communities to consider seeking a milder climate and more fertile lands in the West or South. The Maine Shakers investigated sites

Fig. 4. Maple cheese press, made by Green at Alfred, c. 1875. The press is covered with a thin wash of yellow paint. Height 72¾ inches.

Mountains and two more trips to the seashore, going as far as Kennebunk, Maine, and Rye Beach, New Hampshire (see Fig. 6). His practice was to arrive at a hotel early in the morning, and in the lobby set up his display of fancy goods (sewing baskets, sweaters, candied fruits, and the like) on a folding table, which he had designed and made (Fig. 7). Green's open, straightforward manner made him a good salesman and won him numerous friends among the patrons of the hotels where in later years he became known as "The Old Man of the Mountain."

It is Green's exposure to Victorian furnishings in these stylish resort hotels that undoubtedly accounts for the Victorian appearance of the writing desks he made for the sisters' private rooms in the "fancy" fashion of the day.

During the same period, however, Green continued to make solid bookcases and secretaries more obviously in the Shaker tradition for the public and ministry rooms at Alfred and Sabbathday Lake (Pl. II, Figs. 8, 9). The fact that he made both kinds of furniture simultaneously has caused confusion. One writer erroneously attributed the sister's writing desk shown in Figure 5 to an untalented "hack" (Elder Delmer Wilson) and contrasted it to the secretary shown in Plate II, which she says is the work of an "artist."[7] But the fact is that Henry Green made them both at approximately the same time.

in New York, Virginia, Ohio, and Kentucky. In 1871 the Alfred community was offered for sale both in the United States and in England for $100,000. When no buyer was found, the Alfred Shakers decided to remain and sold valuable outlying timberlands, from which they had long supplied masts and spars to coastal shipbuilding towns. With the rather substantial proceeds of this sale, the Alfred Shakers undertook major improvements which were designed to make the community's life more efficient and more comfortable.

In 1872 the hierarchy of the community at Alfred was reorganized and increased emphasis was put on the making of "fancy goods" for sale to the world. This, in turn, created the need, filled by Green, for more small sewing desks and looms of the kind used by the sisters.

At this time Henry Green took on the additional job of being the salesman for the community. For more than fifty years he made two or three trips each summer to the White

Fig. 5. Sister's writing desk, made by Green at Alfred, c. 1883. Woods are maple, pine, and birch. Height 61, width 31⅛, depth 16 inches.

Fig. 6. Henry Green on his wagon loaded with trunks of Shaker fancy goods starting on one of his summer sales trips to the White Mountains or the seashore. The photograph was taken c. 1890.

Fig. 7. Folding display table with detachable rack, made by Green at Alfred, c. 1880. It is still being used in the gift shop at Sabbathday Lake in the same way Green used it in hotel lobbies during the 1880's. Woods are maple and pine. Height 32, width 32⅜, length (open) 82½ inches.

Fig. 8.   Interior of the secretary shown in Pl. II.

Fig. 10.   Secretary with bookshelf, made by Green at Alfred, c. 1905, for Otis Wallingford, a farm hand at the Alfred community. Stylistically it is earlier than the desk of c. 1883 shown in Fig. 5, to which it is related in form. Woods are oak, walnut, maple, and pine. Height 65, width 38½, depth 17⅜ inches.

Fig. 9.   Bookcase, made by Green at Alfred, c. 1882. The bottom doors open to reveal a set of drawers in the same fashion as the secretary shown in Fig. 8. Woods are birch and butternut. Height 87, width 44, depth 20½ inches.

Green made little furniture after the 1880's (see Fig. 10) although he continued to work in the shop (Fig. 11) making and supervising the making of wood carriers, oval boxes, the bases for pin cushions, rulers, and nests of lapped Shaker boxes (Fig. 12). In 1896 Green became the elder of the church family at Alfred.

Fortunately, the life and work of Henry Green can be documented both from contemporary accounts and by Shakers now at Sabbathday Lake, Maine, who knew him when he and they were at Alfred. Sister Mildred Barker, for example, knew Green for more than twenty-five years and has been able positively to identify over thirty-five pieces of his furniture. Most of this furniture is now at Sabbathday Lake, where it is still being used by the sisters of this last remaining active Shaker community.

Fig. 11. Green with three young assistants in the woodworking shop at Alfred, c. 1900. Note the partially finished oval carriers similar to the one shown in Fig. 12.

Fig. 12. Carrier with handle, pincushion, and six-inch ruler made by Green at Alfred, c. 1910. The carriers, made with birch or maple sides and pine bottoms, were lined with silk and used as sewing baskets. The lining was held in place by ribbons inserted through the small holes in the sides of the carrier.

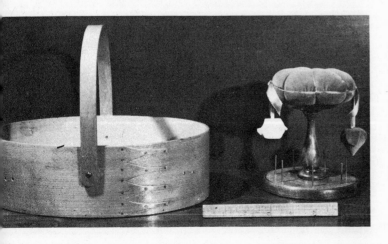

[1] Kate Douglas Wiggin's book about the Shakers, *Susanna and Sue*, published in 1909, was partly written at Alfred.

[2] Margaret Deland set her novel *The Way to Peace* (published in 1910) in Alfred.

[3] "The idea of elevating the sides and back of an ordinary stand or table so that small drawers could be accommodated above the working surface, seems to have originated in the northern New England settlements . . . Alfred, New Gloucester [Sabbathday Lake], Enfield, New Hampshire, and Canterbury." (Edward Deming Andrews and Faith Andrews, *Shaker Furniture*, New Haven, 1937, p. 86.)

[4] A sewing desk made c. 1840 at the New Lebanon, New York, Shaker community appears in Edward Deming Andrews and Faith Andrews, *Religion in Wood*, Bloomington, Indiana, 1966, p. 24.

[5] This appears in the "Recapitulation for 1883" of the Alfred Journal kept by Elder Otis Sawyer. This manuscript journal in the Shaker library at Sabbathday Lake, Maine, contains a number of important references to Henry Green and his furniture.

[6] See R. Mildred Barker, "A History of 'Holy Land'—Alfred, Maine," Part II, *The Shaker Quarterly*, Vol. 3, No. 4 (Winter 1963), pp. 107-127.

[7] "The contrast between the hack and the artist is illustrated by two desks. The desk-on-frame made by Elder Delmer Wilson about 1890 [Fig. 5] ludicrously combines a disproportionately simple case with naive jigsaw whimsies and stock Victorian turnings. The framed construction evidences an elementary approach to cabinetmaking; the case is refined only by the lamb's tongues on the front corners. The desk-and-bookcase made by Elder Henry Greene [*sic*] in 1880 [Fig. 9] exhibits a more sophisticated construction and definition of form. The piece is governed by a sense of proportion; the facade is nicely finished; the bands of molding set up a surface rhythm that helps to reduce the bulk of the case." (Mary Lyn Ray, "A Reappraisal of Shaker Furniture and Society," *Winterthur Portfolio 8*, ed. Ian M. G. Quimby, Charlottesville, 1973, p. 126.)

IV Crafts

In this section on the Shaker crafts we find again, as Dr. Andrews put it precisely, speaking of his friends, the Shakers, that "they animated these materials and made us aware of the kinship between the spirit of the people and the quality of the craft." It is also evident in this section that the communal system, as applied by the Shakers, allowed for personal creativity and inventiveness. The excitement of their craft work derives from the fact that it was undertaken to fulfill a particular purpose. A spiritually-inspired craftsmanship brought the Shaker work to such a height of harmony and usefulness that it has been found difficult to make reproductions today which bear the spirit of the originals.

Eugene Merrick Dodd, the second curator of Hancock Shaker Village after it was saved by Shaker Community, Inc. in 1960, writes here of the Shakers' functionalism and "bare-boned simplicity" and the intimacy of their crafts to their architecture. The fact that everything they needed for daily use was made in the various communities is also interesting, and, although they would buy at times from the World's people, their villages were virtually self-sufficient. Julia Neal takes us further into the many industries of this remarkable sect, and her familiarity with the western and southern communities adds breadth to our survey.

Finally, it is interesting to compare the article written in 1957 by Helen Comstock, long an editor at ANTIQUES, with the material in Section V which brings us up to date on the tremendous rise in international appreciation of the United Society of Believers in Christ's Second Appearing.

Small baskets like these, from the collection of William Lassiter, were made of poplar, larger ones of split black ash. Woven by the sisters at Watervliet, these examples were used chiefly in gathering fruit and vegetables; the very finely woven one (top, left) held knitting. The oval box, of typical form and construction, is of exceptional size: over 23 inches long, 13 inches wide. It came from the New Lebanon Church family and was presented by Mrs. Julia Clough. *Shaker Museum.*

35TH
ANNIVERSARY
ARTICLE

Shaker crafts on view

BY HELEN COMSTOCK

Shaker-made copper kettle and lid, used in making apple sauce or cider; from Canterbury. Width 25 inches. *Shaker Museum.*

BESIDES SUPPLYING ALL THEIR OWN NEEDS, the Shakers developed many products that they marketed outside their communities. Chairmaking was among their earliest industries, begun before 1800, but most widely known after quantity production was effected at New Lebanon (later Mount Lebanon) in the mid-nineteenth century. The Shakers adopted the form of the early eighteenth-century slat back and lightened the stiles and armposts while slightly widening the slat, producing a chair of clean-cut lines and graceful design. The seat was made of woven tapes. Another familiar product from the late 1700's on was the neat oval boxes that the Shakers made in many sizes. Maple was the favored wood for the sides of these, pine for top and bottom, and the "fingers" that formed the side fastenings were secured with copper rivets.

From the shops of the Shakers came innumerable other useful objects, including brooms and brushes, baskets, medicinal herbs and garden seeds, leather goods, silver pens, woven fabrics and clothing, dried sweet corn and apples, kitchen and dairy products, woodwork, shingles, bricks, ironwork, cooper's wares. The Believers were as ingenious as they were industrious, and developed such inventions as the flat broom, the tilting chair, clothespins, the washing machine, and the circular saw.

1957

Small Shaker-made tools. *Top,* a sister's hammer; *center,* a curly-maple mallet; *bottom,* a molding plane. Other objects include bodkins and a paring knife. Buttonholes were made with the small chisel-shape tools at left, and the curved tool at right was used in pressing bonnet pleats. *New York State Museum.*

Tool chest and tool cabinet from the Church family shops, New Lebanon. The Shakers made all types of furniture for their own use as well as the slat-back chairs which they marketed. *Shaker Museum.*

Straw bonnet from Hancock; the bonnet cape, lining, and ribbons are of light blue silk. Such bonnets were woven on a mold with stand, like that seen here. Although bonnets were not made commercially to any extent after the Civil War, they continued to be worn by the sisters. *New York State Museum.*

Bonnet box and sister's blue quilted bonnet *(left),* both from Sabbathday Lake. The black net bonnet over red silk *(center)* represents the extensive bonnet industry of the Church family at New Lebanon which did a thriving business from about 1830 until the Civil War. *Right,* a sister's bonnet of quilted silk, from New Lebanon. *Shaker Museum.*

101

Woolen cloth in checked design, woven at Canterbury. *Left and right,* blue and white; *center,* persimmon red and white. The gift of Eldress Emma King. *Shaker Museum.*

Handkerchief of silk woven in Kentucky, c. 1845. Silk culture was successfully carried out in Kentucky by 1832 and the woven fabric supplied to the northern communities. This is a changeable silk of rose and gray threads; the hem in blind stitching exemplifies the fine needlework of the sisters. *Shaker Museum.*

In this Shaker room, recently installed by the Society of Collectors in Cleveland, the walls are white with peg rail of "Shaker blue" and the floor a reddish yellow. The rockers have New Lebanon stamps, the larger one marked 7; the New Lebanon footstool is upholstered with its original tape in blue and brown. The table, lent by Mr. and Mrs. Ralph Garfield Jones, was made at the North Union community near Cleveland. Hanging on a peg is a man's beaver hat, early nineteenth century. *Dunham Tavern Museum.*

Shaker Museum photographs by Alexander Bender; Dunham Tavern Museum by C. G. Spearman; others, by courtesy of the New York State Museum.

Shaker-made clothes and bonnet rack used at Canterbury. The capes of gray wool were worn by the sisters; a bright red cape among them was made for sale. The three-bar coat hanger, sometimes claimed as a modern invention, is inscribed *1836. Shaker Museum.*

Tailoring counter from Canterbury, with striped woolen cloth (blue, red, and white) from Watervliet. Shears and tailor's basket are Shaker-made; the ruler is inscribed *1845 B W.* The woolen cloth below, in subdued shades of blue and brown, is what the Shakers called their "dressed" cloth, which was glossed with size. *Shaker Museum.*

In spite of the increasing interest in the culture of the Shakers, public exhibits of their crafts are few. Examples from three representative collections are illustrated here; several from a fourth are shown elsewhere in this issue in the article by Dr. Andrews.

New York led the way in preservation for the public of Shaker arts and industries when the New York State Museum in Albany installed a collection early in the 1930's. This consisted at first of material taken from the buildings of the Church family at Watervliet when their property was acquired by Albany County as a county farm. Additions were made from Groveland, New Lebanon, and other centers. In 1933 the museum published a useful handbook of its collection, *The Community Industries of the Shakers,* by Dr. Andrews, which is an excellent introduction to the subject.

Also in New York State is the only museum devoted exclusively to the work of the Shakers, the Shaker Museum at Old Chatham. Here is a collection which John S. Williams has spent more than twenty years in assembling. Opening to the public in 1950, it has since been greatly augmented and at present comprises over nine thousand objects, chiefly from New Lebanon, Hancock, Canterbury, and Sabbathday Lake but representing nearly all the centers. Some recent acquisitions came from Kentucky.

The Society of Collectors in Cleveland recently installed at its Dunham Tavern Museum a Shaker room in which material from Ohio Shakers of the North Union group near Cleveland is combined with Shaker furniture, costumes, baskets, tools, and other objects from New England.

Individual examples of Shaker work are to be seen in other museums but the only other major exhibit we know of which is both public and permanent is at the Fruitlands Museum in Harvard, Massachusetts. Here a house of the Harvard Shakers, built in 1790, has been moved to the grounds and contains a collection of Shaker crafts.

Selected references to ANTIQUES

Material on Shakers published over the years has appeared as follows: *Shaker furniture:* August 1928, pp. 132-136; April 1929, pp. 292-296; December 1932, p. 232; January 1933, pp. 5-9; December 1934, pp. 208-210; November 1935, pp. 204-205; November 1938, pp. 272-273; October 1941, p. 244. *Other Shaker crafts:* April 1938, p. 186; September 1940, p. 126. *Shaker interiors:* October 1936, pp. 162-163; January 1939, pp. 30-32. *General articles and individual items:* November 1947, pp. 356-357; July 1953, p. 56.

Functionalism in Shaker crafts

BY EUGENE MERRICK DODD, *Curator, Hancock Shaker Village*

"THIS PEOPLE ARE strict utilitarians. In all they do, the first inquiry is 'will it be useful?' " This description of the Shakers by David Lamson, an apostate who left the sect in 1845, underscores the reason for the enormous prestige that Shaker artifacts enjoy today. Indeed, the Shakers' artistic achievement is characterized by so unambiguous a utilitarianism that it is a prime expression of what is now recognized as one of this country's most vigorous creative traditions, that of the functionalism pervading our native arts and crafts.

The Shakers' functionalism, which was a direct outgrowth

Shaker stove, from the Mount Lebanon community. A basic version of a familiar Shaker type, this is now in the ministry dining room of the 1830 Brick Dwelling at Hancock Shaker Village. Many of the Eastern Shaker communities had their own foundries, where such stoves were produced. The buildings of the Shakers' Eastern communities rarely contained fireplaces, which the sect regarded as dirty and inefficient, and their stoves were a feature of nearly all their rooms. *Photograph by E. Ray Pearson.*

of their religious beliefs, was a carefully articulated principle. It was also astonishingly prophetic of twentieth-century aesthetics: the words of a Shaker in 1824—"that is best which works best"—would not have been out of place in a Bauhaus manifesto of a century later. Equally precocious were the Shakers' insistence on basic design, scorn for extrinsic decoration, and emphasis on the nature of materials. All these characteristics set the Shakers' artifacts sharply apart from those of their worldly contemporaries. How completely nineteenth-century conventional taste excluded Shaker works from its vision is apparent from Charles Dickens' account of his visit to the Shakers at Mount Lebanon, New York, in 1842: "we walked into a grim room, where several grim hats were hanging on grim pegs, and the time was grimly told by a grim clock. . ." Hawthorne's reaction to the community at Hancock, Massachusetts, which he visited nine years later with Melville, was much the same.

But a century later the Shakers' artifacts were viewed in a totally different light. As the avant-garde in the mid-1920's began exploring the past for a usable tradition which would accord with the high-minded aesthetics radiating from the Bauhaus and other centers of modernism, the Shakers' accomplishment came slowly to be recognized as the purest American statement in the new idiom. It was only a matter of time before artists and designers found in Shaker arts and crafts close analogies to their own artistic ambitions. The artist Charles Sheeler, notably, was decisively affected by the Shakers, as was the Danish designer Kaare Klint, the originator of the modern Scandinavian style of furniture. And it is worthy of remark that the first article on Shaker design appeared in ANTIQUES as early as 1928.

Then, as now, interest in the Shakers was directed primarily to the field of craftsmanship for which the sect is best remembered: that of furniture. But for the Shakers, furniture making was only one craft of many; their passion for self-sufficiency demanded that their manufactures include almost everything required for the conduct of life. Moreover, like the artists and designers of the Bauhaus, they dedicated themselves to the eminently utopian ideal of a planned total environment, every constituent of which should intimately relate to every other. So, for instance, their furniture was an integral part of their buildings—often, in fact, it was actually built in. This remarkable sense of the essential unity of all the crafts, frequently expressed in Shaker writings, extended to almost all of their works, and included, quite as much as their more ambitious undertakings, the small and lowly artifacts which are the subject of this article.

The Shakers' stoves, which were appurtenances of interiors throughout all their communities, may appropriately be considered first, for perhaps no other Shaker craft demonstrates more forthrightly both the geometrical simplicity that functional considerations engender and the sect's instinctive

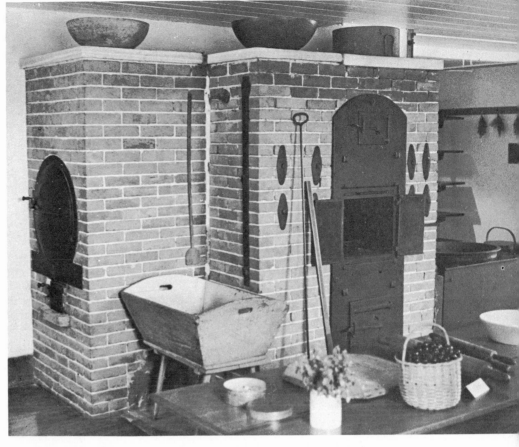

Built-in ovens in the cook room of the 1830 Brick Dwelling at Hancock Shaker Village. To the left is what the Shakers referred to as a "pie oven," an efficient circular oven based on recommendations of Benjamin Thompson, Count Rumford. The built-in kettle to the right, connected by pipe to the village's mountain reservoir, was used for steaming. The Shakers were pioneers in nutrition, and their spacious kitchens were unusually well organized for large-scale cooking. *Photograph by Mark G. Mitchell.*

Handrail of the first meetinghouse of the Mount Lebanon Shaker community, c. 1785. The bold, linear pattern of this rail is characteristic of the Shakers' artistry in wrought iron. *Photograph by the author.*

Foot scraper from the meetinghouse originally built at the Shaker community at Shirley in 1793 and in 1962 moved to Hancock to replace the almost identical meetinghouse which had been built in 1786 and dismantled by the Shakers in 1938. Foot scrapers, a symbol of Shaker cleanliness, are found outside almost every Shaker doorway. Though all of them accord with the Shakers' doctrine of simplicity, they exhibit distinctive regional variations. *Pearson photograph.*

ability to integrate its artifacts with their surroundings. The Shakers must have undertaken the production of stoves within a short time after the establishment of the Eastern communities, for the Reverend William Bentley, on his visit in 1795 to the Shakers at Shirley, Massachusetts, observed that stoves were a conspicuous feature of the meetinghouse, which had been completed two years earlier. At the time, that community as well as those at Mount Lebanon, Hancock, and Harvard had well-equipped foundries, which by the early nineteenth century were almost certainly turning out stoves in some quantity. In basic design these mostly conformed to a standard type: a box stove deriving from the traditional six-plate stove of a much earlier date. The diversity in detail among them, however, is enormous; of the two hundred Shaker stoves which a researcher in the field has recently inventoried, few are exactly alike. Some have straight legs, others have curved or cabriole legs; in some the legs are of cast iron, in others they are of wrought iron with penny feet. While the stoves themselves vary tremendously in size and shape, all reflect the Shakers' insistence on unadorned surfaces (and all exhibit the peculiarity of doors opening from left to right). The stoves of the Shakers' Ohio and Kentucky communities are similar in plan to those of the East, though, like Western Shaker furniture, they exhibit distinctive regional differences. In the main, they are executed with rather less finesse than the Eastern ones, perhaps because they were cast outside the communities: for example, the Aetna Furnace in the Mammoth Cave area of Kentucky was patronized by the Shakers of both Pleasant Hill and South Union during the early years of the nineteenth century.

As impressive in their bareboned simplicity as the Shakers' stoves—and nearly as varied in their details—were the ovens produced for the communal kitchens. Those installed in

1830 in the cook room of Hancock's Brick Dwelling may be taken as representative. A finely designed cast-iron bake oven with an ingenious arrangement of dampers for heat control is flanked on one side by two large iron cooking kettles and on the other by a circular sheet-iron "pie oven." The latter is based on a design of Benjamin Thompson, Count Rumford, which promised a type of even radiation particularly acceptable to the Shakers' sense of efficiency. Conceived in direct response to the demand for functionalism, these specialized ovens and kettles, like the products of so many of the Shakers' workshops, are at the same time dignified and robust, and they are integral parts of the rooms where they are housed.

No less intimately related to their buildings are the wrought-iron handrails and foot scrapers which grace nearly every Shaker doorway. With these, as with stoves and ovens, the Shakers' doctrine of simplicity led to their being derived from a few basic types, but with wide-ranging modifications of detail, for each of the sect's smiths was able subtly to assert his individuality. The result was the creation of a huge variety of forms, some rigidly rectilinear, others almost sensuously curvilinear, though all of them answer practical needs with an inherent rightness and economy and they all provide an aesthetic counterpoint to the clean masses of the buildings whose entrances they adorn.

The Shakers produced countless other metalwares, including most of the tools, machines, and utensils required for their various industries and for their domestic life as well as for sale to the outside world, where their works enjoyed an enviable reputation for excellence. This was notably the case with the Shakers' tinware, which represented an important industry in all their communities. Until the 1850's, tinsmithing was one of the specialized trades for which Hancock was especially well known, and the high-quality products of this

Shaker tin pitcher, probably from the Canterbury community, c.1845. Tinware was produced in all the Shaker communities and was invariably characterized by purely functional lines such as those seen here. *Philadelphia Museum of Art; photograph by A. J. Wyatt.*

Shaker oval boxes. Like most of the Shaker products, the oval boxes were derived from prototypes of a much earlier date, infinitely refined and standardized in Shaker hands. Of pine and maple (and occasionally of other woods), such boxes, usually sold in nests, were among the most popular of all the sect's artifacts. *Philadelphia Museum of Art; Wyatt photograph.*

Shaker oval carrier, probably late nineteenth century. Such carriers, like the Shakers' famous oval boxes, were made in all the Eastern communities from the early years of the nineteenth century. At the Sabbathday Lake community they were still being produced as recently as 1960. *Philadelphia Museum of Art; Wyatt photograph.*

community's tin shop were sold throughout western New England and eastern New York State. Here, as with so many of the Shakers' other crafts, while the designs of their utensils were dependent on the traditional practices brought to the community by the sect's converts, they were invariably simplified and refined in accordance with the Shakers' abhorrence of all superfluities.

Better known today than their metalwares are the products of the Shakers' woodworking shops, where their advanced machinery, much of it operated at an early date by water power provided by their own reservoirs, helped them to turn out a wide array of woodenwares, many of them produced in quantity for large-scale distribution to the outside world. Prominent among these were their boxes, which were made in many sizes and types, including the oval ones for which they are particularly famous. Produced at the Mount Lebanon community at least as early as 1798 and throughout Shakerdom by the end of the first quarter of the nineteenth century, oval boxes were traditionally sold in nests and were available with either a varnished or a painted finish. Usually their bentwood rims, neatly joined by carefully cut "fingers," were of maple, their tops of pine. In their elemental geometry, such boxes are fitting symbols of Shaker design, and, appropriately, they long continued to be a Shaker specialty; the last Shaker brother, Delmar Wilson of

Apple-butter scoop, probably from either the Harvard or the Shirley Shaker community. This 15-inch scoop, carved from a block of maple, illustrates the attention to detail characteristic of even the most commonplace of Shaker utensils. *The Mary Earle Gould Collection, Hancock Shaker Village; photograph by the author.*

Baskets were made in all the Shaker communities in an almost endless range of sizes and patterns. The small baskets in the foreground here were woven of finely cut poplar wood, the larger of split black ash. *Index of American Design.*

the community at Sabbathday Lake, Maine, maintained the industry on a reduced scale until nearly the time of his death in 1961. Other box types, such as the cheese boxes used in the Shakers' highly successful dairy industry, were also produced in some communities until fairly recent times.

During the first half of the nineteenth century, the Shakers of both the Eastern and Western communities manufactured most of the other woodenwares required for their day-to-day routine: bowls, scoops, churns, mortars and pestles, buckets, kegs, and a multitude of others. All are characterized by a clarity of form and modeling of solids and voids which many works of a more sophisticated origin might envy. An apple-butter scoop now at Hancock, but probably originating at either the Harvard or Shirley community, may stand as typical of a whole category of Shaker-made household utensils, for its exquisite shape hewn with remarkable sureness from a single block of maple demonstrates that direct relationship of means to end which is the basis of the functional tradition.

Another important branch of Shaker woodenwares consists of small domestic items designed to be hung from the peg rails which line nearly all Shaker rooms six feet above floor level. "If possible," wrote a Shaker, "everything should be made in such a manner that it may be easily hung." In this they came close to succeeding, for suspensible Shaker artifacts include such disparate items as chairs, clocks, lapboards, clothes hangers, racks, sconces, shelves—an interminable list which helps, perhaps, to explain the presence in one Shaker dwelling alone (that at Hancock) of no fewer than five thousand pegs in its fifty-odd rooms. The character of all these artifacts perfectly accords with that of the rooms where they were used, for they reflect the economy of line, strict geometry, and integrity of craftsmanship discernible in Shaker interior design. Regional variations are evident, too. For instance, the hangable woodenwares produced in the Eastern communities are generally smaller in scale than those of the West, where ampler rooms required larger fittings.

Basketry was another important Shaker industry. "This sect's baskets are unsurpassed in quality," a traveler noted of the Shakers in 1842, and his observation is confirmed by the many well-preserved Shaker baskets which have come down to us. Their variety is as remarkable as the finesse of their execution, their design stringently controlled by the uses to which they were to be put. An account book from the basket shop of the Mount Lebanon community shows that in 1837 at least seventy-six types were produced, ranging from delicate poplar sewing baskets three inches in diameter to split black-ash baskets six feet long for carrying and storing barks, roots, and herbs. As with so many of the Shakers' crafts, their basketmaking techniques derived from inherited practices; in some communities, contemporary accounts inform us, the Shakers learned basketry, along with dyeing methods and herb lore, from neighboring Indians.

Most of the products of the Shakers' crafts were made entirely for their own use. Others, like oval boxes, were made to be sold to the outside world as well, and it was common for each community to specialize in certain industries. Hancock's tinware has already been mentioned; another specialty of the same community was the manufacturing of table swifts, which after 1822 constituted one of its most important sources of income. Like so many of the Shakers' other works, the patterns of these Hancock-made swifts stemmed from those of earlier models but were much simplified for volume production. A Hancock journal of 1835 mentions several "new machines for economically making the ribs of swifts," and the same journal records that year's output of swifts as "over 4000."

The making of swifts persisted as a Hancock industry until sometime after 1865. Well before then, however, it had greatly diminished, and its decline was symptomatic of the fate which befell all the Shaker communities about the time of the Civil War. It could hardly be expected that, as the sect's fortunes dwindled, the Shakers' crafts would retain their vitality, and they did not. Sometimes outward forms remained much the same, as in their chairs and boxes, but there was a marked deterioration in craftsmanship. And sometimes the forms themselves changed—not creatively, as they had in years past, but rather for the sake of change. Their buildings took on touches of Queen Anne here, Ruskin there; Eastlake invaded their furniture. There was now in nearly all their crafts a note of artistic pretentiousness, a lamentable relaxing of their old standards.

Only a few crafts were continued into the twentieth century. These were mostly industries dependent on painstaking handwork. Shaker cloaks, which were fashionable among the well-to-do in the early years of the present century, were produced at Canterbury, Sabbathday Lake, and Mount Lebanon; sewing baskets, often covered with a delicate material woven from thinly cut strips of poplar wood, were familiar wares at New Hampshire and Maine seaside and mountain resorts, where they were sold by the Shaker sisters; and many an early twentieth-century child must have received a Shaker-dressed doll. But by then the creative years of Shaker craftsmanship had passed, and the sect's principles of functionalism and simplicity were being freshly discovered and applied by others.

Table swift made at the Shaker community at Hancock, where swift making was an important industry until about 1865. Produced in large quantities, such swifts were widely sold throughout the eastern United States. They are made of wood, usually stained yellow. *Henry Francis du Pont Winterthur Museum.*

Shaker sewing basket from the Sabbathday Lake community, c. 1900-1910. Such baskets, lined with silk and outfitted with a pincushion, needle case, emery, and wax, were popular items made by the Eastern Shakers until fairly recently. Other sewing baskets were covered with a material woven of thin strips of poplar wood. *Henry Ford Museum.*

Shaker industries in Kentucky

BY JULIA NEAL

Fig. 1.   Centre Family House at the South Union, Kentucky, Shaker community, built between 1822 and 1833. It was the dwelling house for the church family. *Except as noted, photographs are by Helga Photo Studio.*

EXACTLY TWO HUNDRED YEARS ago, when the first settlers were coming into the "District of Kentucke," a group of nine Shakers left England for the American Colonies. After establishing eleven societies in the East, the Shakers gathered two communities in Kentucky. The Pleasant Hill society in Mercer County, first known as Shawnee Run, was established in December 1806. The following October, the second society was formed on the Gasper River in Logan County, and was later called South Union. Both societies were located on lands given by the first converts, as the societies in the East had been. Those who lived at some distance would sell their holdings and move to

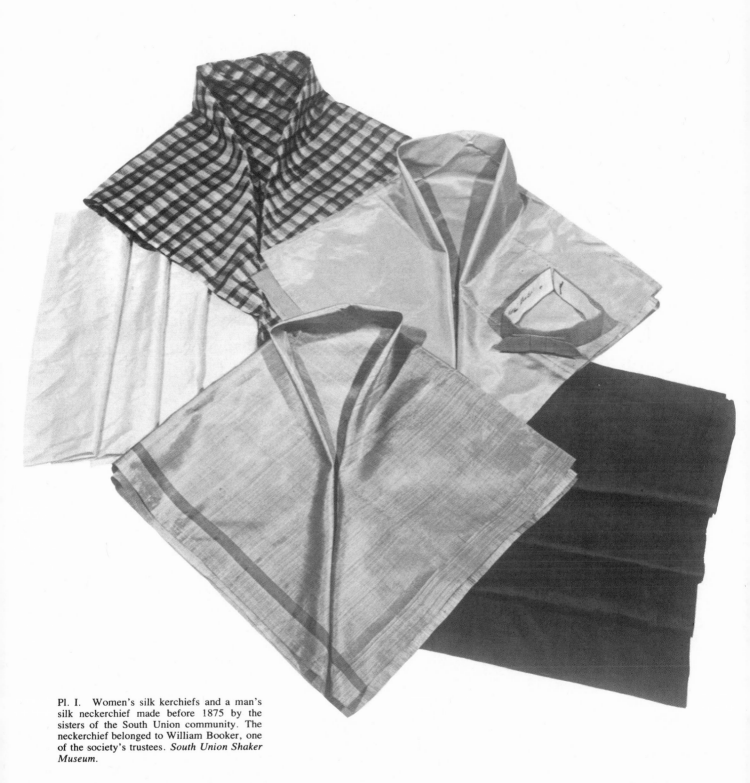

Pl. I. Women's silk kerchiefs and a man's
silk neckerchief made before 1875 by the
sisters of the South Union community. The
neckerchief belonged to William Booker, one
of the society's trustees. *South Union Shaker
Museum*.

Facing page.

Pl. II. Dining table at Pleasant Hill laden with food grown and prepared at the community.

Fig. 2. This building, in which the hides were tanned at the Pleasant Hill community, was built in 1823.

Fig. 3. View from the dining room into the kitchen at the Pleasant Hill Centre Family House. The arch is a familiar design in Kentucky Shaker architecture.

the community, contributing their money and movable possessions to the church. Most of the additional lands that were purchased had to be cleared before being planted. Roads had to be cut, wells dug, and fences built. But communal effort soon resulted in fields of corn and wheat, flax and hemp, in productive gardens, and in young orchards of apple, peach, cherry, pear, and plum trees. The frame buildings first put up were replaced in a few years by large, carefully built Georgian structures of brick or stone (Fig. 1). Shops and mills (Fig. 2) were built with the same expert craftsmanship as the larger dwellings and the meeting house. A distinctive feature of Kentucky Shaker design is the arch, which was used in both exterior and interior construction (Fig. 3).

The orderly, quiet, and prosperous appearance of the Pleasant Hill and South Union Shaker villages soon set

114

Fig. 4. Seed box and seed papers from the South Union community. *South Union Shaker Museum.*

a high standard for what was still rather rough frontier country. Although the combined annual membership of Kentucky's two Shaker towns never reached one thousand, the Shakers exerted a disproportionate influence on the agricultural and industrial life of the state during the nineteenth century.

Long before there were commercial seed companies the American Shakers were selling packaged garden seeds. The first out-of-state selling trip recorded at South Union took place in 1821 when "Eli McLean and Isaac Choat went to Clarksville [Tennessee] and other places with a two-horse wagon load of garden seed."[1] Soon the Kentucky Shakers began flatboat trips along the rivers as far south as New Orleans. The horse-drawn as well as the water-borne seed merchants each took with them several thousand papers full of seeds to retail to individuals, and a number of wholesale boxes which were packed with a varying number of seed papers. These boxes were left with customers and the unsold papers taken up the next year.

Readying the seeds for market required making wooden boxes, cutting and, on a small hand press, printing labels and seed papers, filling the papers with cleaned seeds, and packing the boxes (Fig. 4). By the middle of the nineteenth century the seed business of both Kentucky societies had grown to be their most profitable industry. They were in demand throughout the South, and gardens as far away as Mobile, Alabama, and Houston, Texas, were sown with Kentucky Shaker seeds.

Fig. 5. Straw bonnets and the tools to make them from the South Union community. The bonnet at the left has a silk tail, the one at the right a patterned cotton one. The bonnet mold is of cherry. The object in the foreground splits the straw. The hinged top of the splitter closes over the wire needles through which the flattened straw is drawn. *South Union Shaker Museum.*

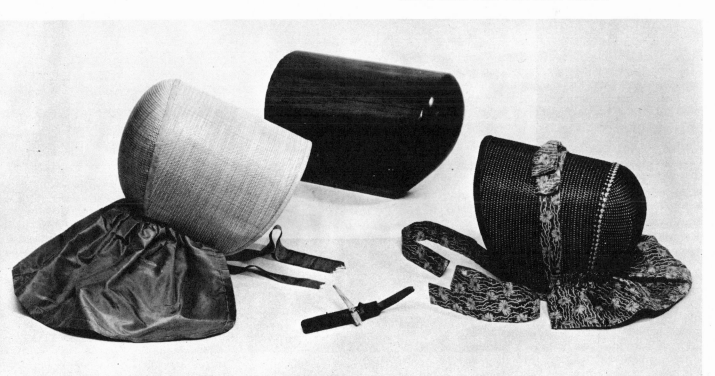

A kindred industry was the production and sale of dried herbs and other medicinal plants. Pleasant Hill marketed hyssop, pennyroyal, thyme, sweet balm, and others. South Union dealt in lobelia and stramonium and sold barrels of sage in nearby Bowling Green. Some of the herbs were taken on the seed trips, along with carpeting, half-bushel measures, baskets, gauging rods, books, brooms, onions, women's straw bonnets, and men's straw hats.

The men's hats were made by fastening together hand-braided lengths of straw. Straw for women's bonnets was woven on machines invented by the Shakers. The bonnet chips, or parts, were cut from the web, dampened, and then allowed to dry on a shaped wooden block (Fig. 5). Afterwards the chips were joined together with a straw braid or strip of cloth and a small wire was attached to help hold the shape of the bonnet. Rye and oaten straw were preferred, but any hollow straw that could be flattened and split into narrow strips was gathered from the field, being cut "just above the upper joint on the stock."[2] The straw was scalded and placed in the sun to bleach before being woven or braided. Some of the late bonnets were made of palm leaves, an art learned from the New York sisters.

The tools for bonnet making, like those essential to other Shaker handicrafts, were made by the societies' workmen. In July 1835, for example, the South Union journal records that Samuel S. McClelland made new worsted combs so that the sisters could comb out the wool of the "Bakewell" and Merino sheep that cropped the community's fields (Figs. 6, 7).

The celibate Shakers played an important role in building up purebred stock in Kentucky, for cattle breeding was one of the earliest ventures at both societies. Shaker cattle were shown at fairs where they won blue ribbons, and where sales were made. The brethren at Pleasant Hill separated cattle pastures from cultivated fields by building some forty miles of remarkable stone fences "laid up without mortar or footing"[3] (Fig. 8). The account books and family journals of both Kentucky societies showed a steady income from cattle sales because full-blooded Shorthorns were in demand not only in Kentucky but also in Indiana, Illinois, Tennessee, and Mississippi, and later in Kansas and Texas. After the Civil War, soldiers from both armies returned to the Kentucky societies to buy cattle.

The Shakers were expert horticulturists, who practiced scientific grafting so that some variety of fruit was nearly always available for sauces and pies as well as for drying, canning, and preserving. Preserve houses, called preservatories, and drying houses were built so that sisters could process the fruit without disrupting the regular cooking of meals. The fruit season lasted from the cherries and strawberries of early May to the pears and apples of late autumn. During the season the work was constant, putting up both the societies' fruit crops and those of neighbors as well. One reads in the account books of 111 barrels of cider pressed in one day, or 3,917 jars of strawberry preserves made in ten days—a major undertaking when all the work was done by hand. Wines and cordials were made for sale or were kept for medicinal purposes. Apple butter and tomato preserves were also sold.

The coming of the railroad helped expedite the shipping of the heavy wooden cases of preserves. The glass preserve jars, embossed with *Shaker Preserves* or *Shaker Preserves, South Union* were brought to South Union by the carload from St. Louis or Cincinnati, where they were made (Fig. 9). Before the jars were packed the women covered the

Fig. 6. The journal of the South Union community relates that on July 28, 1835, Samuel S. McClelland was making worsted combs, and that on the twenty-ninth the sisters were making silk kerchiefs (from Journal A, Vol. 2). *Western Kentucky University, Kentucky Library.*

Fig. 7. Worsted combs with reinforcing brass plates referred to in the Journal entry illustrated in Fig. 6. *Western Kentucky University, Kentucky Museum.*

Fig. 8. Some of the forty miles of expertly built dry stone wall at the Pleasant Hill community.

Fig. 9. South Union preserve jars, the labeled top of a wooden crate in which they were packed, and a tool for tightening jar tops. *South Union Shaker Museum.*

tops with tin foil.

The Shakers also sold potatoes, both Irish and sweet, home-baked bread, cheese, flour, sweet potato plants, and dressed turkeys. Beginning in 1854 the Kentucky societies started a chicken business, specializing in the Light Brahma and Partridge Cochin breeds, of which Elder Hervey Lauderdale Eads of South Union (Fig. 10) wrote, ''the Light Bramahs take the palm.''[4]

Silk culture was one of the most unusual Shaker industries in Kentucky. Journal references indicate that it flourished between 1825 and 1875. A visitor to Pleasant Hill in 1825 reported that the silkworm was reared there and that ''sewing silk of superior quality is made of its web.''[5] In 1873 when Elder Henry C. Blinn of the Canterbury, New Hampshire, society visited Pleasant Hill he was interested in seeing the wound cocoons. At South Union he was given a cocoon and an oval box containing spools of colored silk thread (see Fig. 11) to show the sisters at Canterbury.

On New Year's Day, 1832, the South Union sisters all appeared dressed in their homemade silk kerchiefs for the first time. The following New Year's the sisters gave a

117

DOERR.   *H. L. Eads*
          80 yrs old   12TH & MARKET STS.
                                LOUISVILLE, KY.

Fig. 10. Hervey Lauderdale Eads (1807-1892), photographed in 1887. He served as elder of the South Union community from 1836 to 1892, and was appointed head elder of the Kentucky bishopric when it was formed in 1868. *Western Kentucky University, Kentucky Library.*

"beautiful silk neckerchief" to each of the brethren. The men's neckerchiefs were collar width, fastened in the back, and had a small bow at the front. The women's kerchiefs were thirty-two- by thirty-four-inch hemmed rectangles. The colors ranged from white, blue, pink, and mulberry to light and dark brown. Some kerchiefs were irridescent, others were checked, and still others had a border of a contrasting color or a border design made by heavier threads (Pl. I). Many of the kerchiefs were sold or sent as gifts to the Eastern societies. Men's white silk handkerchiefs were also made and sold at $1.00 each.

For several years in the 1840's the Shaker community at North Union, Ohio, sent their cocoons to be reeled at South Union "where they are skilled in the art."[6] Finally two South Union sisters went to North Union to teach the reeling and spinning of silk.

To review the industries of the Kentucky Shakers is to understand why Shaker leaders would say "an idle lazy person will not long abide in the society." If utopia had been attained at either of the Kentucky Shaker communities, it would have been brought about through work—not idle dreams.

[1] Journal A of the South Union Church family, Vol. 1, p. 310.

[2] Marywebb Gibson Robb, *Shakerism in Kentucky*, Lexington, 1942, p. 94.

[3] S. W. Thomas and J. C. Thomas, *The Simple Spirit*, Pleasant Hill, 1973, p. 99.

[4] Journal B of the South Union Church family, Vol. 2, p. 209.

[5] Heartman's Historical Series, No. 22, *Letters on the Condition of Kentucky*, ed. E. G. Swem (reprinted from *Richmond Enquirer*, April-May, 1825), New York, 1925, p. 65.

[6] Caroline Piercy, *The Valley of God's Pleasure*, New York, 1951, p. 109.

Fig. 11. Oval box containing spools of colored silk thread made by the Logan County Shakers. *Philadelphia Museum of Art, gift of Mr. and Mrs. Julius Zieget; photograph by A. J. Wyatt.*

V   Continuing the Shaker Tradition

In "Shaker Crafts on View" (*see* p. 100) Helen Comstock writes that "in spite of the increasing interest in the culture of the Shakers, public exhibits of their crafts are few." In this article, written in 1957, she mentions New York State as leading the way in preservation by having installed a collection as early as 1930 in the State Museum in Albany, about which a useful handbook was published in 1933. Entitled "The Community Industries of the Shakers," it was written by Dr. Andrews. Also at this early date John Williams was busy collecting the furniture and crafts of the Shakers in Old Chatham, New York.

By 1970 Williams was able to show the public thirty-six galleries housing 17,000 objects of Shaker design and manufacture. The situation described by Helen Comstock had thus greatly changed. During his years of collecting Williams also assembled one of the most extensive libraries relating to the Shakers. There are a number of other museum collections of Shaker artifacts not housed in the buildings of former settlements. A list of these, and of Shaker settlements, follows at the end of the general introduction (pp. 7-8).

Of the public museums special mention should be made of Hancock Shaker Village, just west of Pittsfield, Massachusetts. Acquired by a non-profit foundation in 1960 under the aegis of Mrs. Lawrence K. Miller, many original Shaker buildings have been painstakingly restored and now house one of the finest and most extensive collections of Shaker craftsmanship. The settlement is as it was when occupied by the Shakers, and some of its physical features are unique, to wit, the great round stone barn. Here also exist a fine library and one of the most extensive collections of inspirational drawings. An increasing number of people visit the village each season. The attendance record of 1976 shows a total of 48,738 visitors. Another public museum is Pleasant Hill in Kentucky, opened in 1962. This village, preserved by Earl D. Wallace, is almost entirely as it was originally. There also exists a Shaker Room in the American Museum at Bath, England, carrying back to England lasting evidence of the freedom for her inspiration that Mother Ann Lee found in America. In recent years there has been a marked increase in the exhibition of Shaker artifacts in Europe as well as in this country.

The Shaker movement has always been well documented, but more pertinent publications are now available. Among these we make special mention of a book, prepared in 1976, by John Harlow Ott, the present curator of Hancock Shaker Village. This is not only a guide to the Village but an excellent background survey of Shaker culture. A second publication of special value to students of the Shaker movement is *Shaker Literature, A Bibliography,* compiled and annotated by Mary L. Richmond, in two volumes, *I. By the Shakers,* and *II. About the Shakers.* This has been published by the Shaker Community, Inc., Hancock, Massachusetts, and is distributed by the University Press of New England, Hanover, New Hampshire.

Unfortunately, Shaker culture has become reduced to that which can be preserved in the form of artifacts. For today there are only ten Shakers living, four at Sabbathday Lake in Maine, four at Canterbury, New Hampshire, and two in Vermont. Of the four at Canterbury, two are eldresses: Eldress Bertha Lindsay and Eldress Gertrude Soule, originally from Sabbathday Lake. Canterbury Shaker Village has become Shaker Village, Inc., a non-profit, charitable organization, because the Canterbury sisters are dedicated to seeing that their heritage is preserved and available to the public when they themselves are gone. The village is still owned by the Shaker society and a board, director, and financial director join the Shaker eldresses in making decisions.

The Shakers today

BY BARBARA SNOW DELANEY

THE SHAKERS HAVE BEEN the subject of thousands of words—spoken and written—for almost two hundred years. The curious have long enjoyed Shaker hospitality and even now can find a few hours of calm and peace in talking with the sisters and visiting the buildings and grounds of the two remaining Shaker communities. Remote from metropolitan centers, these last two living Shaker villages were among the earliest "gathered into gospel order." Canterbury, New Hampshire, had been started on land given by Benjamin Whitcher in 1782; Sabbathday Lake at New Gloucester, Maine, in the same year. The earlier buildings of both communities reflect the New England architecture of the post-Revolutionary period. A number of them are illustrated here, and a view of Canterbury is shown on the cover.

Today Canterbury and Sabbathday Lake are open to visitors and have museums and gift shops. The sisters say that among the most responsive guests are young people from colleges, both nearby and abroad. There is no generation gap here: the simplicity and beauty of the Shakers' way of life appeals as perhaps never before.

In their own writings the Shakers have told their story

Eldress Bertha Lindsay and Sister Lillian Phelps on the porch of the Trustees' Office at Canterbury, which was built in 1831 "of hand-made bricks and roofed with Welsh slate—the first introduced in N.H." (Sister Aida Elam, *History of the Shakers,* Canterbury, New Hampshire, 1962.) *All photographs are by Miller/Swift.*

The Enfield Sisters' Dwelling at Canterbury was built in 1826 as the Trustees' Office of the (Canterbury) North Family and was moved to its present location in 1917. Beyond is the vast main dwelling: "Our main dwelling, erected in 1793, consists of 56 rooms. The upper floors furnish airy sleeping apartments and our chapel. On the basement level is our kitchen. . . Our Family Dining hall once easily accommodated 60 persons at one sitting, and when I came to the Shakers we had two well-filled sittings. Low-backed chairs, that could easily be pushed under trestle tables, were used. The table service at that time was of iron-stone-china, made especially for us, in England." (Sister Aida, *op. cit.*)

The Whitcher House (c. 1780), Canterbury. "It was here, before our family organized, that Benj. Whitcher for 10 years, housed and fed 43 Shaker converts. Most of our buildings are on part of this original property of 100 acres." (Sister Aida, *op. cit.*)

The Great Barn at Canterbury (1856), "a substantial structure with feeding floor 250 ft. long and hay lofts to hold over 400 ton of hay. It once housed over 100 head of registered Guernsey stock, and in years past sheltered 20 yoke of oxen for heavy farmwork." (Sister Aida, *op. cit.*)

better than anyone else, and some of these writings are quoted in the captions here. Another expression of the Shaker point of view is given in these words of Eldress Bertha Lindsay of Canterbury, published in a brochure titled *Industries and Inventions of The Shakers:* "Some have asked—why did the Shakers invent so much—why did such beauty abound in their work—I can only say—The beauty of the world about us is only according to what we our-selves bring to it. For example: to some, Autumn is a prelude to winter with its cold and loneliness. To others, Autumn represents the magnificence of God's Great Creation . . . with you and only you, lies the choice . . . I like the words of the poet, who looking on the beauty of Autumn, said, 'Dear Lord, when with this life I'm thru and I make my abode with you, Just one thing I would ask of Thee. Will Heaven have Autumn, and crimson trees?' "

Left to right: the Brethren's Shop, the Carriage House, and the Carpenter's Shop at Canterbury. In the distance is the Horse Barn built in 1819.

The School, built in 1823. "Through the years of school-room experience, Shaker teachers have accented individual teaching rather than large classes. . . . As years passed, the time spent in the school-room increased to six hours a day, and thirty-six weeks a year." (Sister Miriam Wall, *Education and Recreation,* Canterbury, 1962.)

The Children's House (1810), where the girls adopted by the Canterbury society lived (the boys lived in another building, no longer standing). Some of the children came with parents who joined and others came as orphans to be brought up by the Shakers. Their presence gave a true sense of family to the community. "On Christmas morning the young people greeted the family, as they assembled for breakfast, with a beautiful Christmas Carol. One especially impressive and original arrangement, was called 'The Celestial Choir.' As the family assembled for breakfast a small group of singers started singing on the attic stairs, and, as they descended, others joined them on each loft, resulting in a full chorus of voices, as they approached the lower hall . . ." (Sister Lillian Phelps, *Shaker Music,* Canterbury, 1962.)

The Sabbathday Lake community in 1850.
Ink and water-color drawing by Joshua H. Bussell of Alfred, Maine.
Sabbathday Lake collection.

NOVITIATE ORDER, POLAND HILL.

EVERTS & PECK, PUBRS.   "SHAKER VILLAGE," VIEW FROM THE NORTH WEST, WEST GLOUCESTER, MAINE.   (Nº 2 CEMETERY.)

The Sabbathday Lake community in the late 1800's. Lithograph published by Everts & Peck.

The Ministry Shop at Sabbathday Lake, built in 1839 to accommodate the Maine ministry.

Herb House (1824), Boy's Shop (1850), and Office Woodshed (1816) at Sabbathday Lake. Boys lived in the shop until their mid-teens under the supervision of the brethren, learning wood- and metalworking. The upper stories of the woodshed were used for a variety of crafts.

Brick Dwelling House (1883-1884) at Sabbathday Lake, where the sisters live today. A drawing of the community in 1850 shows an earlier building on this site which appears to have been somewhat similar. The style suggests the large brick-and-stone dwelling houses of the Kentucky Shakers. In the sisters' waiting room here are the *Rules for Doing Good:* "Do all the good you can/ In all the ways you can/ To all the People you can/ In every place you can/ At all the times you can/As long as ever you can."

The Shaker communities

This list is based on one in *The Shaker Adventure* by Marguerite Fellows Melcher (Cleveland, 1941), emended with the kind assistance of contributors to this issue and of Robert F. W. Meader, director of the Shaker Museum at Old Chatham, New York.

Community	Organized	Disbanded	Present status of property
Watervliet, New York (Niskayuna)	1787	1938	Part occupied by county institution and airport, part privately owned
Mount Lebanon, New York (New Lebanon)	1787	1947	Part occupied by private school, part privately owned
Hancock, Massachusetts	1790	1960	Restoration open to public
Harvard, Massachusetts	1791	1919	Privately owned; one building moved to Fruitlands Museum
Enfield, Connecticut	1792	1917	Part occupied by state institution, part privately owned
Tyringham, Massachusetts	1792	1875	Privately owned
Alfred, Maine	1793	1931	Occupied by religious organization
Canterbury, New Hampshire	1793		Still occupied by Shakers
Enfield, New Hampshire	1793	1918	Part occupied by religious organization, part privately owned
Sabbathday Lake, Maine (Poland Spring)	1793		Still occupied by Shakers
Shirley, Massachusetts	1793	1908	Occupied by state institution
West Union, Indiana (Busro, near Vincennes)	1810	1827	Site built over; no Shaker buildings left
South Union, Kentucky	1811	1922	Part occupied by religious organization, part privately owned
Union Village, Ohio	1812	1910	Part occupied by religious organization, part by state institution, part privately owned
Watervliet, Ohio (Dayton)	1813	1900	Part occupied by state institution, part privately owned
Pleasant Hill, Kentucky	1814	1910	Restoration open to public
Whitewater, Ohio	1824	1907	Privately owned
Groveland, New York	1826	1892	Occupied by state institution
North Union, Ohio (Cleveland)	1826	1889	Site built over; no Shaker buildings left

Index